# The

# Silent Power

### Selections from

*The Mountain Path*
and
*The Call Divine*

SRI RAMANASRAMAM
Tiruvannamalai
2004

First Edition   : 2002 (1000 copies)
Reprint         : 2004 (1000 copies)

ISBN  81-88225-49-5

Price: 1'5    ‑
CC No: 1009

*Published by*
V.S. Ramanan
President, Board of Trustees
Sri Ramanasramam
Tiruvannamalai 606 603
Tamil Nadu
INDIA
Tel: 91-4175-37292
Fax: 91-4175-37491
Email: alagamma@vsnl.com
Website: www.ramana-maharshi.org

*Designed and typeset at*
Sri Ramanasramam

*Printed by*
Sudarsan Graphics
27, Neelakanta Mehta Street
T.Nagar
Chennai 600 017

# FOREWORD

Like the previous volumes *Fragrant Petals* and *Surpassing Love and Grace*, *The Silent Power* contains selections from *The Mountain Path* and *The Call Divine*. Besides the writings on Sri Maharshi and his beloved Arunachala, a few other interesting articles on various topics have been included.

TIRUVANNAMALAI                    **V.S. RAMANAN**
15 FEBRUARY 2002                PUBLISHER

# CONTENTS

# PART I

# ON ARUNACHALA

# ARUNACHALA

## Lucia Osborne

*"Arunachala! Thou art the inner Self who dances
in the Heart as 'I'. Heart is Thy name, O Lord!"* (Five
Stanzas to Sri Arunachala, *verse 2.*)

IN THE *PURANAS* Arunachala is referred to as the oldest
Hill on earth and is regarded as the heart of the Universe.
Scientists have also pointed out the eastern ghats of the Deccan
plateau as the oldest land. Arunachala has many names:
*Arunagiri, Sonagiri, Sudarsanagiri, Annamalai,* to mention but
a few and is also referred to as the *Tejolingam* — the *lingam* of
effulgence — which is the formless emblem of Siva.

The form of the Hill is said to resemble *Sri Chakra,* the
emblem of the Cosmos with its substratum, and *shaktas* regard
this Hill as *Sri Chakra* itself. Bhagavan took an active part in the
installation of *Sri Chakra* in the temple dedicated to the mother.

Devotees of Siva consider this divine Hill as the form of
Siva, who appeared in the midst of Brahma and Vishnu as a
column of fire without beginning or end in order to dispel their
ignorance. Both failed to realise his presence by their physical
efforts. This signifies the inability of mind or intellect to go
beyond itself. Arunachala is traditionally identified with
Sudarsana (a form of the *chakra* or discus of Vishnu). In the

form of a deity, Sudarsana appears in a fierce aspect, armed with weapons of destruction. When a seeker penetrates beyond the semblance of the terrible, while struggling to overcome what seems terrible in himself — namely, the dark downward propensities of his own psyche — grace reveals itself as love and compassion. This, according to Dr. Mees, an authority on symbolism, is the etymology of Sudarsana which aims at the destruction of these propensities, so as to reveal love and beauty.

Many saints and sages have sung and composed songs in praise of Arunachala and its import, and some have attained enlightenment here. Shankara also seems to have visited Arunachala. In one of his compositions he calls this Hill 'Meru' and says, like Bhagavan, that *Sidddha Purushas* are found here. Saint Namasivaya lived in one of the caves, which is still called by his name. His disciple has written the well-known *Annamalai Venba*, a hymn in praise of Arunachala. Another well-known Saiva saint, Virupaksha, also lived in a cave higher up on the slope. It is said to be in the shape of OM — and some devotees have heard there, the sound of OM in silent meditation. The saint's tomb is also there and this cave bears his name. Bhagavan spent seventeen years in it and later moved up to Skandashram where a trickle of water changed overnight to a perennial stream whose water, like that of the Ganges, does not deteriorate with time. Arunagirinathar, another notable saint, is also celebrated for his songs of praise after he received illumination through the grace of Muruga in the Arunachala temple.

When mention was made one day of the tank adjoining the Ashram being called Agastya Thirtam, the Maharshi was asked if that sage ever visited the Hill. Bhagavan remarked "Yes, of course, everyone must come here eventually", meaning that everyone must eventually return to the source — Arunachala.

Sages have said that one can attain salvation by being born in Tiruvarur, by dying in Benares, by worshipping in Chidambaram and by merely thinking of Arunachala. "So worship Arunachala of shining golden lustre for mere remembrance of Him ensures deliverance,"[1] Bhagavan also affirms.

Bhagavan mentioned that the Hill is one of light. Sometimes one can see manifestations of lights on the Hill. In the early years, a French devotee, Sujata Sen, once spent the night on the Hill in protest against an order of the management not allowing women devotees to remain in the Ashram after dark. This was the most wonderful time for many devotees when Bhagavan used to sit with them for an hour or so in radiant silence. Sujata dwelt on her grievance one-pointedly. Next morning she told me that she was taken inside the Hill and found a whole world in it, which she described. I did not pay much attention to this, dismissing it as a dream or imagination. Strangely enough many years later, in 1970 to be precise, another devotee, Mr. S. N. Tandon, had a similar experience which he described in detail in the April 1970 issue of *The Mountain Path* in 1970, that year. It is reminiscent of Dante's inferno, leading by stages to light, in which all manifestation disappears in the feeling of pure I-Am-ness.

Sri Visvanatha Swami, who from his adolescence spent many years with Bhagavan, shares with us the following account. Bhagavan said to him one day in the early twenties, "Innumerable are the visions I have had of this Hill, Arunachala. I have seen beautiful groves of trees and fine palaces inside it. Once I saw a large tank and a big congregation of *rishis* and yogis seated on a

---

[1] *Five Hymns on Arunachala.*

wide plain around it. Every face was familiar and so were the surroundings. A dais was there and I went up and sat on it with my right hand held up in *Chin-mudra*. It seemed my usual place and my usual pose." *Chin-mudra* is a pose in which the right hand is held up with the thumb and forefinger joined and the three remaining fingers straight up. It is the pose of Dakshinamurti. It denotes the unity of the individual with Brahman, the transcendental Reality beyond the three *gunas*.

It is said in the *puranas* that a *Siddha Purusha,* the ancient teacher in the form of an eternal youth, is present higher up on one of the slopes seated under an enormous banyan tree, diffusing his spiritual radiance in silence.

In the early days Bhagavan used to roam a good deal on the Hill. One day he found, in a dried up watercourse, a banyan leaf of such enormous size that it set him wondering what tree could produce such a leaf. Proceeding further he saw from a distance a huge banyan tree growing on what looked like sheer rock. Going closer, Bhagavan inadvertently put his foot in a hornet's nest and did not withdraw it until the hornets appeased their anger for being disturbed, by badly stinging his leg.

Bhagavan did not go near the tree but returned to his abode. Subsequently he firmly discouraged devotees from trying to find the place saying that it was inaccessible and not advisable for them to do so. "It is impossible. I know it!" he told them, "For there shall no man see Me and live." (Exodus 33, 20).

The finite ego must die before it can behold and merge with infinity. Once a whole group of devotees, obviously unaware of Bhagavan's injunction, set out to locate the place but they found themselves in such distress that all they could pray for was to be able to return safely!

Any endeavour to write about Arunachala is like 'painting the lily' — to borrow an apt expression. It is impossible to present it better or more clearly than Bhagavan himself and in this case there is no distinction between them. Arunachala in the form of Bhagavan speaks about himself! Like Bhagavan, the Hill comes to life and can appear to us as the beloved of our heart as an indescribable tenderness. What could be nearer and dearer than one's own Self, Arunachala?

"O nectar springing up in the heart of devotees .... haven of my refuge. . ." (*Arunachala Padikam*).

"The one Self, the sole Reality alone exists eternally. When even the youthful teacher of ancient times, Dakshinamurti, revealed it through speechless eloquence, who else could convey it by speech?" (*Ekatma Panchakam*).

Bhagavan explained that the Universe is like a painting on a screen, that screen being the red Hill, Arunachala. That which rises and sinks is made up only of what it rises from. The finality of the Universe is Arunachala. Meditating on Arunachala or the Self, there is a vibration 'I'. Tracing the source of 'I', the primal 'I-I' alone remains and it is inexpressible. The very first *sloka* in the *Marital Garland of Letters* expresses this tersely: "Arunachala! Thou dost root out the ego of those who meditate on Thee in the Heart, O Arunachala!"

Bhagavan, who scarcely ever gave advice to devotees unless asked, wholeheartedly approved and encouraged their going round the Hill as conducive and very beneficial to progress in *sadhana*. He himself set an example by doing *giripradakshina* countless times. Worship is expressed by going around the object of worship in silent remembrance or singing *bhajans* — and not giving way to stray thoughts. One usually goes barefoot. The most auspicious times are full-moon days, Sivaratri (the night of Siva) and Kartikai, the night when the beacon is lit on top of the Hill. It is said that the pilgrim is accompanied by an invisible host of *siddhas* and *rishis*. On festival days, the stream of pilgrims in white and brightly coloured clothes resembles garlands of flowers, strewn around Arunachala, wafting their scent in the way of *bhajans*.

Among the many holy places in India, representing different modes of spirituality, Arunachala stands out as the centre of the most direct path, guided by the silent influence of the guru. It is the centre and the path where physical contact with the guru is not necessary. The silent teaching acts and speaks directly to the Heart. There was something essentially immutable and rocklike in Bhagavan, although he had a thousand faces. He spoke and explained when asked, but his greatest and most inspiring teaching was, like the Hill, like Dakshinamurti, given in silence. Through Bhagavan, the immense potentiality for spiritual regeneration inherent in Arunachala, with which he identified himself, was brought to life and into focus.

The benedictory verse adopted as an auspicious introduction to the *Five Hymns to Sri Arunachala* was rather puzzling as it was not clear who actually wrote those words "the *Paramatman,* who is the same as Arunachala or Ramana." Sri T. P. Ramachandra Iyer, one of the oldest devotees, who gave up his practice as a lawyer to serve Bhagavan, was consulted and so was Sri Visvanatha Swami. Their account of the matter is that one day, when Bhagavan went out of Virupaksha Cave for his usual morning walk, one Amritanatha Yati put on Bhagavan's seat a piece of paper on which he told in a Malayalam verse, of his great longing to know who Bhagavan really was, "Are you the manifestation of Lord Vishnu, or Siva, or the great grammarian Vararuchi, or the greatest of *yatis* (renunciates)?"

His question was couched in classic form and script. When he returned a little later to the cave, he found Bhagavan already back from his walk. On the reverse of the piece of paper was Bhagavan's reply, also in verse and Malayalam script, rendered with mastery. On reading it, Amritanatha Yati felt shaken and in all humility fell at Bhagavan's feet "like a tall coconut tree cut even at the base", to use his own words.

The reply was as follows: "In the lotus-shaped Heart of all, beginning with Vishnu, there shines as absolute Consciousness the *Paramatman* who is the same as Arunachala-Ramana. When the mind melts with love of Him and reaches the inmost recess of the Heart wherein He dwells as the beloved, the subtle eye pure intellect opens and He reveals Himself as pure Consciousness."

"Through the potent grace of Bhagavan", wrote Osborne, "the path of Self-enquiry was brought within the competence of men and women of this age, was indeed fashioned into a new path that can be followed in the conditions of the modern world with no form or ritual . . . . This creation of a new path to suit the needs of the age has made Arunachala the spiritual centre of the world. More than ever, now that he has shed his physical body and is one with Arunachala, the grace and guidance that emanates from him to those who turn to him and seek his aid is centred outwardly at Arunachala, to which many are drawn, both those who were disciples of Bhagavan in his lifetime and those who have come later."

As in the lifetime of Bhagavan, so also now one can turn and speak to Arunachala-Ramana far more effectively than in one's own words, by repeating an appropriate verse chosen from the *Five Hymns to Arunachala* which Bhagavan wrote on behalf of his disciples from whom he was not separate. The individual, being only a mode of absolute Consciousness, struggles against his finitude to regain his primordial state of absolute freedom through grace. These verses come from the devotees' own heart:

"Even when the thieves of the five senses break in upon me, art Thou not still in my Heart, O Arunachala?"

"On seeking Thy real Self with courage I lost my moorings. Have mercy on me, O Arunachala!"

"Unless Thou extend Thy hand of grace in mercy, I am lost, O Arunachala!"

"Unlovable I am to look at now, yet ornament me with Thy grace and then regard me, O Arunachala!"

"Thou hast administered the drug of confusion to me, so must I be confounded! Shine Thou as grace, the cure of all confusion, O Arunachala!"

"Lord! Who art Consciousness itself reigning over the sublime Sonagiri, forgive the grievous wrongs of this poor self, and by Thy gracious glance benignant as the rain cloud, save me from being lost once more in the dreary waste, or else I cannot ford the grim (stream of universal) manifestation."

"Lord! Deign to ease me in my weariness struggling like a deer that is trapped. Lord Arunachala! What can be Thy will?"

"O pure One! If the five elements, the living beings and every manifest thing is nothing but Thy all-embracing light, how then can I alone be separate from Thee . . ."

Bhagavan has given many indications of his continued presence. Ever-present, all-pervading, where could he go? Outwardly manifested and visible as the Hill, he will remain here always, guiding as before. "Only the body travels the Self just is", Bhagavan used to say. His body travelled and disappeared. He just is as he always has been and the visible support of grace is Arunachala. It is a great blessing to be able to come here, to stay here. After many years, every day still seems like a gift. One cannot help feeling the living presence, radiation and powerful spiritual help accorded to those who seek it, and above all are humble enough to surrender to this influence of faith!

"The Hill which draws to itself those who are rich in *jnana tapas* (those who are ever intent on gaining wisdom) is this Arunachala" (*Annamalai Venba*).

಍ ಎ

# ARUNACHALA'S TRUE SHAPE

## Aquarius

*From every angle Arunachala presents a different aspect. But the Sivalinga, representing the Hill, symbolises its true shape, that of the formless including all forms.*

ARUNACHALA IS RAMANA. Every true devotee of Sri Bhagavan comes to feel this to be true. Arunachala is an insentient Hill while Sri Ramana was a sentient human being. How could they be the same, we ask, except perhaps in a metaphysical sense? But do we know what Arunachala is like even in the physical sense?

I approach Arunachala generally by bus from the east as I come to Tiruvannamalai from Madras. Arunachala becomes visible from about ten miles away. At first it is only a vague cloudlike shape but as I come nearer it becomes clearer. It assumes the form of an irregular cone somewhat longish at the base with a curved spur on its northern side.

This shape lasts only until I come to the temple of Arunachaleswara. It changes gradually when I proceed to the Ashram and finally when I reach the Ashram it assumes the beautiful shape which is familiar to all devotees of Sri Bhagavan. It reminds me of Mount Kailas as it looks in the familiar photographs of that sacred mountain. Others have also noticed this resemblance.

I have seen Arunachala not only from these two angles but also from numerous other angles too. While going round the Hill on the holy circuit it looks different from each spot.

Names like the 'five-faced Arunachala' and the 'four-faced Arunachala' have been given to those aspects in which it appears to possess five peaks or four peaks. When one comes to the northern side the appearance changes completely. It becomes more rugged and massive. Arunachala has many faces and many shapes. From every angle it presents a different aspect, reminding us of the ever changing flux of creation, the motionless dance of Arunachala-Siva whose unity penetrates all diversity!

Every true devotee of Siva believes that Arunachala, the Hill, is Siva himself or a huge Siva *linga* in the form of the Hill. The *puranas* elaborate this. That is why one walks round it barefoot reverently all the eight miles of the way. Siva *linga* is simply an emblem of Siva, in its manifest form as the Hill and the *linga* of fire without beginning or end, as mentioned in the well known story of its first appearance, symbolises its unmanifest transcendence. Thus Siva is *rupa* (with form) and *arupa* (without form). He has many forms and at the same time can reveal himself as formless.

"When I approach regarding Thee as having form, Thou standest as a Hill on earth. If (with the mind) the seeker looks for Thy (essential) form as formless, he is like one who travels the earth to see the (ever-present) ether. To dwell without thought upon Thy (boundless) nature is to lose one's (separate) identity like a doll of sugar when it comes in contact with the ocean (of nectar) and when I come to realize who I am, what else is this identity of mine (but Thee), O Thou Who standest as the towering Aruna Hill?"[1]

---

[1] *Arunachala Ashtakam*, verse 3.

# THE CULT OF THE HILL

## Kenneth Grant

OF THE OUTER symbol of Sri Arunachala on earth, Lord Siva says, "Meditate on the fact that in the heart of the Hill surges the spiritual glory, within which the whole world is contained."

It is in fact this holy Hill — the Mount Kailas of the south and the very embodiment of Siva — that is the manifest and visible guru of Bhagavan Sri Ramana Maharshi.

It behoves us therefore to remember, that now the beloved master is not with us any more in the fleshy garments of frail humanity, this holy guru is nonetheless visible and accessible to all those whose eyes are opened to the spiritual glories which Siva describes as surging within its mysterious heart.

Here is the tangible focus of that tremendous spiritual energy, which burned with unabated strength in the form of Ramana; thus is this symbol supremely sanctified for us today by the certainty of liberation, which Bhagavan himself taught was the reward of the unflinching surrender of the ego in the flames of its all consuming embrace.

Those who feel disturbed within themselves at the great loss of the body of Bhagavan, should instantly direct their minds to the contemplation of the 'Hill of the Holy Beacon', which — Bhagavan has told us — only waits to respond eagerly and tenderly to even our weakest yearnings towards It.

In his article called 'Physical Supports of Grace', Arthur Osborne says that the Hill called Arunachala is verily the greatest of physical supports, for did it not bear upon its sacred surface the earthly tabernacle which was the physical form of Bhagavan?

Yet for those who are unable to live within sight of the earthly Arunachala, there need be no regrets, for the Hill itself is but a thought-construction same as any other. If we would grasp the inner significance veiled by the 'dull', outer form of its simple contours, we must search within the heart, and establish contact with that regionless bliss, void of all conceptions which the mind is capable of formulating. For Arunachala is the symbol of the void nature of the Self manifesting in so simple a shape as the 'Hill of the Holy Beacon'.

This is the form of Ramana, which lasts longer than the human garment that he wore for our sake. But as long as the world appearance lasts for each aspirant, so will endure the Hill, to symbolise to us the perfect void, the all full Self that lies as the heart in the spaceless and timeless eternity.

Sri Ramakrishna Paramahamsa said,

"Is Kali, my divine mother, of a black complexion? She appears black because she is viewed from a distance, but when intimately known she is no longer so. The sky appears blue at a distance but look at it close by and you will find that it has no colour. The water of the ocean looks blue at a distance, but when you go near and take it in your hand, you find that it is colourless."

And so it is with the 'Hill of the Holy Beacon'; go near to it in spirit and it is without shape, without colour, without attributes of any kind. It is only distance which lends it the illusory qualities it seems to possess. Really, we impress the void — It essentially is with the attributes we seem ourselves to possess and then we imagine seeing what is not truly there. Thus it is our attributes we have to slough if we would come close to the sacred symbol and know its real significance, and our everyday life can help us insofar as we regard all things that occur to us in a new light. For instance, instead of viewing circumstances and conditions as isolated phenomena occurring to us for no reason at all, we should strive to regard each event as a stone upon the slopes of Arunachala; each trivial repetition of which event constitutes at last that sacred 'mount of the spirit' which is our true nature. Thus we can worship Sri Bhagavan in and through our ordinary mundane life. It is merely a matter of re-orientation and determination to accept as deeply significant in a spiritual way all the seemingly trite and disconnected incidents which constantly occur to us. Yet is this but a preliminary to the final process of knowing Truth as it really is? For when Arunachala has been thus truly built into the fabric of our hearts, we shall need to view each separate part no longer as a separate stone of the divine edifice, but as the structure entire in its sublimely simple shape of the 'holy Hill'. And then, entering into the heart thereof with understanding, we shall know the whole as the embodiment of that spirit of grace and compassion which eternally enlightens our hearts.

In this way it is possible for the less advanced of us to perform a spiritual discipline while living in the world even though far removed from the outer symbol of divine grace in Tiruvannamalai.

It is only when we realise that it is we who clothe the formless Arunachala with form, because we view it with the eyes of the body, that we shall begin to search within our hearts for the formless Reality which that form veils. Until then, we shall not penetrate and comprehend this miracle, nor shall we understand why Bhagavan Sri Ramana made no difference between his human form and his Hill form. It is the guru in hill form who is an everlasting beacon of hope for those who inhabit the earth (or body). As soon as the body is dissolved into a shining mist, so also does the guru's Hill form dissolve, and we are no longer deluded by other concepts such as our own form or the Hill form — for these twain are no more. The underlying Reality shines forth as the pure and perfect void, conceptless and ever blissful.

As an aid to the realisation of this, it may help the devotee — if he be remote from the physical sight of the Hill — to create a mental picture thereof and endeavour through such a *mandala* to pervade the Hill and become one with it. Certain physical supports, such as a mound of actual stones taken from the Hill itself, may further the project and intensify the concentration, and also link the devotee in some subtle manner with the focus of spiritual peace abiding in Tiruvannamalai.

Yet all this is of no avail if it be not always borne in mind that these accessories are but props for exalting the consciousness to the pitch necessary for contacting the subtle emanations of grace, which spring from the spaceless Arunachala Siva, whose eternal abode is the Heart. For, all takes place in, and is supported by, the void, of which the Hill itself is the perfect and singular symbol.

CB EO

# PART II

# ON BHAGAVAN

PART II

ON BHAGAVAN

# Sab Jan, Sri Maharshi's Classmate

## "SEIN"

B HAGAVAN SRI RAMANA MAHARSHI emphasised several times that the holy Hill Arunachala is the heart of the world and the most ancient and oldest of hills. He also used to say that it is a natural Sri Chakra and that from each angle it has a different appearance. That is why it is a Siva *linga* with form and without form. From every direction it presents itself in a different majestic posture.

And so also I always like to see Sri Maharshi from different angles and enjoy the differences in his appearances! In respect of his teachings, movements in the Ashram, like assisting in the kitchen, catering to the needs of devotees and even dumb animals, devotees know Bhagavan to be more as one's own father and mother and God incarnate, than as *Tatwama Sivaroopa*. His greatness as an intimate friend of a classmate of his is portrayed here truly revealing his loving heart.

When young Venkataraman (of Tiruchuzhi) was reading in Madurai in the American Mission High School, in his 4th, 5th and 6th forms, he was closely associated with one Muslim boy, whom he chose as his intimate friend. Venkataraman was very fond of this young Muslim, whom he addressed as Sab Jan. His real name is M. Abdul Wahab.

Mr. Wahab, now a retired police inspector, nearing eighty, unable to see or hear properly, is living with his son at Neyveli. Upon hearing this, I went there to meet with him. He welcomed me very kindly and I was amazed at the serenity of his face. I requested him to tell me something about Bhagavan in his school days. His talks on the Maharshi gave me a thrilling experience and enabled me to visualise with the mind's eye, the intimate friendship that he enjoyed with Venkataraman, later to be known as the great Sri Ramana Maharshi.

When I asked him to describe the depth of their friendship, Mr. Wahab recalled his happy past and jumped with joy saying, "We were inseparable mates." This Muslim enjoyed such privilege with young Venkataraman. He began to tell me of his past happy days that he was fortunate enough to spend with him.

"Venkataraman was very learned in Tamil and he stood first in the class. When the teacher wanted to refer to some portion in the text book he used to ask Venkataraman to quote and Venkataraman used to do it with remarkable clarity. He was particularly well-versed in *Nannool Soothram* (Aphorisms of Tamil Grammar). Our Tamil Pandit, Mr. John Balakrishnan, was very fond of him. His knowledge of Tamil was really remarkable and that of Tamil Grammar very exact.

"But Venkataraman was not very good in English, in the sense that he was not an expert in that subject. In other subjects also he was above average. But in general, he was not much interested in his school books. He was very fond of playing games and among games he was an expert in football. He used to encourage me to join him in playing the game, saying that he would teach me how to play. We used to play together in the same team and I was particular only to be with Venkataraman. As was usual in those days, in Brahmin families they did not encourage the boys taking part in games, so Venkataraman's relatives did not like his playing games.

"Once when we were playing football, Venkataraman, while defending against the attacks of the opposing players, received a severe knock on his right leg, which immediately got swollen. He was frightened and had to return home and I carried him to a hospital and had some medicine applied and brought his leg to normal condition. He was very happy and thanked me for the timely help.

"Even as a student he was very religious. Every Saturday and Sunday he would go to Tiruparankunram and go round the Subramania Swamy Temple with fervent religious ecstasy. He used to take me several times with him and make me go around the temple saying, 'God's creation is alike and there is no difference in creation. God is the same, the apparent differences in Gods are created by man.' In the company of Venkataraman I never felt any difference between a mosque and the Subramania Swamy temple.

"This instruction of his really implanted in me a better understanding of the secret approach to religion and thenceforth I never felt any difference between a Hindu God and any other God. It is quite possible, in fact, I am very certain, that because of such an universal outlook implanted in me by Venkataraman in those days, in my later days I could become an ardent devotee of Sri Varadaraja Perumal of Kancheepuram, who actually enveloped me in his divine rapture. I had visions of Varadaraja Perumal in dreams and they proved to be of great help to me."

When I asked him in what manner, he said, "For 12 years I was able to partake actively in the *Garuda seva* of Sri Varadaraja Perumal by giving a shoulder to lift the deity of Perumal, while going in procession in the streets of Kancheepuram, which I regard even today as the greatest privilege and boon. There arose some complication also since some *Vaishnavites* objected to my carrying the deity since I was a Muslim and that was settled amicably later. This service of 12 years to Varadaraja Perumal made me cling to him closer and closer.

"Once when I was on duty in Kuppam I received a telegram that my wife, of whom I was extremely fond, had had an abortion and I was greatly worried that she would die. The same night Sri Varadaraja Perumal appeared in my dream and assured me that my wife was all right and I need not worry. When I returned to Tirupathur she was in normal condition. Her recovery was the grace of Sri Perumal."

Mr. Wahab then spoke about Venkataraman:

"Suddenly Venkataraman disappeared and it was a shock to me that he did not even tell me about his running away from his home. His disappearance made his mother terribly sorrow-stricken. While I refer to his home and his mother, 1 can not but mention the kindness and love with which mother Alagammal used to receive me.

"Some Saturdays and Sundays he would go to Tiruchuzhi to be with his mother and kith and kin. I would also go there to see him. Mother Alagammal would immediately, with all affection, tell Venkataraman of my arrival saying, 'Your dear Muslim friend has come.' She had a wonderful face beaming with nobility. Every time she gave me a very good reception and used to give me whatever eatables were prepared at home. If by chance 1 did not turn up for one weekend, she used to enquire about my absence and give Venkataraman the eatables saying: 'Give these to your Muslim friend'. I could never forget the maternal love of Alagammal and her kindness to me, even though I was a Muslim." (Muslims were regarded by caste

Brahmins as untouchables in those days. They were despised and treated with contempt.)

I asked Sab Jan, "When did you know of the whereabouts of Sri Maharshi?"

He said, "I was enlisted in the police department and in 1903 in one of the medical shops at Uttaramerur, I was surprised to see a portrait of Venkataraman but completely different in appearance. I was anxious to know how the shop man happened to possess the photo of my classmate. Then I was told that this was the 'Brahamana Swamy' living in Tiruvannamalai and that the Swamy was in *mounam* then.

"I was very eager to meet Venkataraman and at last after several months of strenuous efforts, I was able to come to Sri Ramanasramam, the abode of Sri Maharshi, my dear friend of those earlier days. I entered it and was taken in by a cowherd woman who was supplying milk to Bhagavan. I introduced myself as his classmate 'Sab Jan' (but his facial expression clearly showed that he had at once recognised me and that my introduction was not at all necessary) and he was pleased to receive me although he did not speak. He simply nodded his head with a radiant face. I was thrilled to meet my classmate as a swamy for he was all the more beautiful and resplendent, with a mark of saintliness.

"Again, I went there when I was the Inspector of Police at Tirupathur. I was very sad then, since my father had passed away but Bhagavan showed me his mother's tomb, which consoled me. I understood from Bhagavan's action that death is inevitable as far as the body is concerned and that no one was ever born or died. He was so kind and offered something to eat and asked me to stay for a couple of days but I could not, since I was on duty. After that I went to see him several times and on all occasions he showed special attention to me and introduced me to whoever was present on the occasion with deep love and kindness. He used to make me sit by his side while taking food in the dining hall, which later I came to know was quite unusual with him.

"A sudden change took place in me. I was transformed into a devotee of Bhagavan from being a friend of Venkataraman. This inward change brought about by Sri Maharshi is the greatest boon he has showered on me. He showed his greatness once through a dream in which he showed signs of my wife passing away and in a mysterious way consoled me and prepared me for the shocking incident. It did take place very soon and my beloved wife passed away as predicted and by the grace of Sri Maharshi it did not affect me very much. This attitude of detachment is itself the grace of Bhagavan.

"In 1950, on 14th April, the memorable day of his *Brahma Nirvana*, it so happened that even though it would have been absolutely impossible for me to come to Tiruvannamalai, as I was on duty at a place far away, I had the opportunity of visiting the Ashram. In the day time I could not take my food due to lack of time during travel to go to a hotel and take food.

"I paid my homage to my friend and guru who left his mortal coil that night, but whose presence still pervaded his abode. I was in deep mourning. Then someone asked me to take food since I looked fatigued and tired and it was late in the night. I flatly refused saying, '1 am going to fast the whole day as an act of reverence and homage to my intimate friend and revered guru.' "

I thanked Mr. Wahab and took leave of him with great reverence as the classmate of Bhagavan who did not stop at being a classmate but went further and understood Venkataraman as Bhagavan Sri Ramana Maharshi, the *Maha Guru.**

---

* Sri Wahab has passed away since the article was written.

# KRISHNAPREM AND
# MAHARSHI

## Marie B. Byles

*(An English professor in the* purvasrama, *Sri Krishnaprem was an orthodox devotee of Krishna and as such had no intention to follow Self-Enquiry. Yet he had a striking experience of the significance of the question, 'Who am I?', when he visited Bhagavan for his blessings.)*

SRI KRISHNAPREM, formerly Professor Ronald Nixon from Cambridge in England, had taught literature at Varanasi and Lucknow universities before he gave up the life of the world, donned the *gerua* robes and became a *sannyasin*. He took as his guru the saintly woman Yashoda Mai who had been a leader of Indian social life before she became a *sannyasini* and established an ashram at Mirtola, about eighteen miles from Almora in the Himalayas. Here Krishnaprem took up his abode, soon performing the *Vaishnava* rituals in the temple, and, when the Brahmin cook left, doing the cooking also. When Yashoda Mai died in 1945 he was left in charge of the ashram, though he handed over the management to another in 1955, ten years before his own death.

He was an orthodox *Vaishnava* and worshipper of Lord Krishna, that is, of the personal aspect of the Supreme, and the last thing that would have entered his head would have been to find his goal through asking the question, 'Who am I?' However he regarded Maharshi as a living shining light of India and because of this in 1948, he made the long journey from Almora to the south to receive his blessing. The story of his visit is told by his friend, Dilip Kumar Roy, in his book about him. And as I do not seem to remember having read about this visit elsewhere, others may find it as illuminating as I do.

He entered the room where Maharshi was reclining with devotees before him, and sat down among them to meditate. As soon as he did so, he heard a voice saying over and over again, 'Who are you? Who are you? Who are you?' He tried to ignore it but eventually he replied silently, 'I am Krishna's servant.' The voice still went on relentlessly. The question changed to, 'Who was Krishna?' He answered, 'Nanda's son', and formulated various other answers, 'He is an Avatar, the One-in-all, the resident in every heart'. The voice continued asking the former question. He became very disturbed, and finally he rose and left the room. He returned and the voice continued as before. Silently he prayed to Radha for guidance, but she shook her head. Then the answer was revealed, but how we are not told!

In the morning he again sat down with the other devotees. Maharshi gave him a lightning glance and smiled at him. He closed his eyes, then on a sudden impulse he found himself silently asking Maharshi his own question, 'Who are you?' Something made him open his eyes. Maharshi's couch was empty, there was no Maharshi on it. He closed his eyes again but in a moment opened them. Maharshi was reclining in his usual place and he gave a fleeting smile and meaningful glance, after which he looked away. Maharshi did not ask Krishnaprem to cease from worshipping Lord Krishna and surrendering all to him.

He never did this, there are different ways for different temperaments. Some will perhaps be more direct than others, but in the end all will find the same answer, and that vacant couch gives the answer better than all.

And this is what I was taught when invisible cords drew me to the Maha Bodhi Meditation Centre near Mandalay in Burma. I was told there, that many are the ways of learning *Vipasana* or insight meditation, but that all end up with the experience of *phyit pyet* (come- go or ceaseless change) or the end of 'I' and 'mine' and 'me' — you are not the worrying thoughts that disturb you, you are not the mind, you are not the body. What are you then? *phyit pyet.* Whatever is your way or my way, it is always helpful to understand and appreciate the ways of others, as for example that of Krishnaprem, who found that ultimately all faded away and there was only Krishna.

C3 80

# A PERFECT IMAGE
# OF THE LIFE DIVINE

## K. Ramachandra

SAINTS AND SAGES are the salt of the earth. They are the saviours of humanity. They are the sustainers of society. Philo remarks, "Households, cities, countries and nations have enjoyed great happiness, when a single individual has taken heed of the good and beautiful. Such men not only liberate themselves, they fill those they meet with a free mind."

In all sects of Hinduism, the worship of saints and sages forms an important feature. In the galaxy of spiritual giants of modern India, a great Sage answering to the description of Philo in a supreme way is Bhagavan Sri Ramana, popularly known to the world as 'Maharshi'. He stayed at Tiruvannamalai in South India for over fifty four years and attained *Mahasamadhi* in April 1950.

His teachings have a unique appeal to thinkers of both east and west. He was considered as the living embodiment of God-centred life, a perfect image of the life divine in the mirror of human existence. In the words of the world-renowned psychoanalyst, Dr. Carl Jung, "Sri Ramana is a true son of the Indian earth. He is genuine, and in addition to that, something quite phenomenal. In India, he is the whitest spot in a white space."

The Maharshi was not one of those teachers who tried to make an impression on his devotees and others by mystifying matters. Nor did he utilise any of the psychic powers to attract the curiosity-seekers and miracle-mongers. His method was direct. He disclosed the truth in the simplest possible language, as realised and lived by him. He spoke very little, but in his look there was not only love and compassion, but a subtle spiritual vibration which went deeper into the heart of the visitor.

He regarded nothing as alien, none as other, no event as undesirable. He thought of others in the same way as he thought of himself. Love and love alone influenced his relationship with others. His teaching through *mouna* or silence was difficult to be understood by the average person. Once a visitor from the west put the question to him as to why he was staying at one spot for years together, without moving about and preaching to people the truth he had realised. The Maharshi gave his characteristic reply as follows:

"How do you know that I am not doing it? Does preaching consist in mounting a platform and haranguing the people around? Preaching is simple communication of knowledge. It can really be done in silence only. What do you think of a man who listens to a sermon for an hour and goes away without having been impressed by it, so as to change his life? Compare him with another who sits near a holy presence and goes after some time with his outlook on life totally changed. Which is better, to preach loudly without effect or to sit silently sending out inner force?" On another occasion, answering a similar question by an Indian devotee, he remarked,

"Vivekananda was perfectly right when he said that if you thought a good thought in a cave it would have repercussions on the whole world."

So, let us meditate in silence on Bhagavan Sri Ramana.
Though he has given up his physical body, his presence is felt
by thousands as before. It is not confined to Tiruvannamalai. It
never was. But the hall where he sat for years has a special
attraction. Visitors come there even today from the four corners
of the globe.

ର ଧ

# A Talk with Sri Ramana Maharshi

## Pryns Hopkins

IN AS MUCH AS India is notoriously the most metaphysically minded of all countries, it was natural that I should seek discussions in this field.

Ever since I had read Paul Brunton's *A Search in Secret India*, I had been keen to visit Ramana Maharshi, the sage whom Brunton found most impressive of all those he sought out. Soon after my arrival at his Ashram, I bade one of the two men who mainly ministered to him to inquire whether I might ask two questions. Accordingly, I was requested to take my seat in front of the group of visitors and an interpreter sat next to me (although Maharshi usually gets queries directly through English) and was invited to present my question.

The first of these questions was: "If it is true that all the objective world owes its existence to the ego, then how can that ego ever have the experience of surprise as it does, for example, when we stub our toe on an unseen obstacle?"

Sri Bhagavan answered, 'that the ego is not to be thought of as antecedent to the world of phenomena, but that both rise or fall together. Neither is more real than the other, only the non-empirical Self is more real. By reflecting on the true nature of the Self, one comes at length to undermine the ego and at the same time, material obstacle and stubbed toe are equally unreal and to dwell in the true reality which is beyond them all.'

He then went on to outline that we only know the object at all through sensations derived from it remotely. Moreover, that physicists had now shown that in place of what we thought to be a solid object there are only dancing electrons and protons.

I replied that while we had, indeed, direct knowledge only of sensations, we know less, for all that knowledge about the objects which gave rise to the sensations, about which knowledge was checked continually by making predictions, acting on them and seeing them verified or disproved. Furthermore (here I went on to my second query), "If the outer phenomena which I think I perceive have no reality apart from my ego, how is it that someone else also perceived them? For example not only do I lift my foot higher to avoid tripping over that stool yonder, but you also raise your foot higher to avoid tripping over it too. Is it by a mere coincidence that each of us independently has come to the conclusion that a stool is there?"

Sri Maharshi replied that the stool and our two egos were created by one another mutually. While one is asleep, one may dream of a stool and of persons who avoided tripping over it just as persons in waking life did, yet did that prove that the dream stool is any more real. And so we had it back and forth for an hour, with the gathering very amused, for all Hindus seem to enjoy a metaphysical contest.

During that afternoon's *darshan* I again had the privilege of an hour's talk with Maharshi himself. Observing that he had given orders to place a dish of food for his peacock, I asked, "When I return to America would it be good to busy myself with disseminating your books to the people just as you offer this food to the peacocks?" He laughed and answered that if I thought it good it would be good, but otherwise not. I asked whether, quite apart from whatever I thought, it wasn't useful to have pointed out a way to those who were ripe for a new outlook. He countered with "Who thinks they are ready?"

The Maharshi went on to say that the essential thing is to divorce our sense of self from what our ego and our body are feeling or doing. We should think "Feelings are going on, this body is acting in such and such a manner", but never "I feel, I act." What the body craves or does is not our affair.

I then asked, "Have we then no responsibility at all for the behaviour of our ego?"

He replied, "None at all. Let it go its own way like an automaton."

"But", I objected, "you have told us that all the animal propensities are attributes of the ego. If when a man attains *jivanmukti* he ceases to feel responsibility for the behaviour of his ego and body, won't they run amok completely?" I illustrated my point with the story of Dr. Jekyll and Mr. Hyde.

Maharshi replied, "When you have attained *jivanmukti,* you will know the answer to those questions. Your task now is not to worry about them but to know the Self."

But I am forced to doubt the whole theory unless it explains away this discrepancy. "Here before us is the Maharshi who has attained *jivanmukti,* and so withdrawn from all responsibility for the conduct of his ego and the body we see before us. But though he declares them to be the seat of all evil propensities, his ego and body continue to behave quite decorously instead of running wild. This forces me to suspect that something in the hypothesis is incorrect."

He answered, "Let the Maharshi deal with that problem if it arises and let Mr. Hopkins deal with who is Mr. Hopkins."

# RAMANA REMINISCENCES

## I

### Arthur Osborne

ONCE AGAIN PEOPLE throng together from all parts of India for the *jayanti* of Bhagavan Sri Ramana Maharshi at Tiruvannamalai, at the foot of the sacred mountain of Arunachala. Men and women, young and old, from the town dweller in coat and trousers, to the old- world type of sadhu, all alike irrespective of wealth and caste and from beyond India also. America, France, England, Holland, Poland, Iraq, Ceylon, all are represented. The Maharshi, tall, white-haired, golden-hued, frail now beyond his years, goes through his daily routine unperturbed, unselfconscious because completely Self-conscious. Being unperturbed does not mean being indifferent. Never was a face so alive, so responsive. From the rocklike gravity of *samadhi* to free laughter or amused smile; the gracious recognition of a devotee drawn here again, a smile, a look of compassionate understanding that enters the heart and makes an impression never to be forgotten. Nevertheless, many are puzzled about the Maharshi.

They ask, is he always in *samadhi*? Is it true that he will not answer questions? Will he give advice? What kind of *sadhana* does he enjoin? Is it any use for ordinary people to go there? I will try to answer these questions as well as I can.

The supreme and final state of *samadhi* is *Sahaja samadhi* which does not imply any trance or any oblivion to what we ignorant ones call the 'outer world'. There is no going backward and forward between the trance state and the mental state, the inner and the outer. His consciousness embraced both constantly without distinction and without effort. That is why the Maharshi seems so natural, so simple and human in his ways, why he laughs and talks freely and shows interest in all that goes on around him. He is gracious to all, responds to all. There is no aloofness, except the indefinable grandeur, the awe that a devotee feels in his heart.

He does not expound doctrine unless asked, but when asked, he answers all sincere questions graciously and often at length. The widespread idea that he will not answer questions perhaps comes from his own saying that he teaches in silence. But that only means that the real teaching is the silent influence on the heart of the seeker. The doubts of the mind can take shape in words but that is not the essential teaching because, however much a man may argue, he is not really to be convinced in his mind but only in his heart, and that teaching is silent. Indeed, it has happened to many, as Paul Brunton relates, that when they sat silent before the Maharshi such peace flooded their heart that the mind's doubts also disappeared and they found they had no questions to ask.

In any case, the kind of *sadhana* enjoined by the Maharshi requires little philosophy. It is the pure doctrine of *Advaita*. This is the most direct spiritual path and is generally referred to in books as the path of intellect. It is a peculiar use of the word intellect and misleads many. It does not mean that there must be more attention given to philosophy, but only that there must be understanding of the one simple, central truth of *Advaita*, that the Self alone is, and that all that is real in you is the Self, *Atma*, and is universal. Therefore, the Maharshi does not answer questions about what you were before you were born or what you will be after you die. All such philosophy is brushed aside and he turns you from such mental speculation to the practical work of Self-enquiry 'Who am I?' When asked about life after death, he has said, "Why worry about what you will be when you die? First find out what you are now." Probably commentators will arise who will call this 'agnosticism' just as some have called Buddha an agnostic or atheist, but it is not. It is simply a practical reminder that the Self not only was or will be, but is and that if the apparent separateness of this life is an illusion, that of the next life is also, and for the *jnani* who abides in truth, in the Self, there is neither past nor future, neither birth nor death, neither this life nor the next. The body may change, but the consciousness of Self is immutable.

In order to realise universality, it is necessary to try to give up the thought 'I am this' or 'I am that' and think only 'I am'. That is why the Maharshi does not advise people to change their conditions of life or work. If he advised them to give up their work or their family and retire into solitude it would only be exchanging the thought 'I am a house-holder' for 'I am a *sadhu*' and both are equally wrong, since it is necessary to remember only 'I am'. It is the mind that must be overcome, and that can be done as well in the world as in the jungle. If a man's work distracts him from *sadhana*, the cure is not to give it up (because even if he does other thoughts will distract him) but to ask himself constantly

'Who am I?' 'Who is doing this work?', until he acquires detachment towards his life just like the work of the bank cashier who receives and pays out lakhs of rupees efficiently and without emotion because he is not the owner and the sums do not affect him. It means playing one's part in life with the same consciousness and indifference to the outcome as the actor who knows that he himself is not affected whether he has to play Caesar who is stabbed or Brutus who stabs.

Many will say that this is too hard. Certainly it is harder to control the mind than the body. To fast or remain celibate is much easier than to keep your mind off food or women. But if the way is hard, the blessing and support of the presence of Bhagavan on earth is great. If a man says that this *sadhana* is beyond his power, he is quite right! If he says that it is beyond the power of Bhagavan to enable him to follow it, he is wrong. Some may also say that it is a cold and mental way, but it is not really. It is not a *sadhana* of the mind but of the heart. The mind may wander and argue, the heart can perceive the truth of oneness and must hold grimly to it until the wandering mind has been subdued. But how can one explain the conviction that awakens in the heart and the remembrance that stays there from sitting in the presence of the Maharshi? His eyes can destroy doubt and implant the seed of life. The memory is in the heart, not the mind. It must be experienced to be understood.

Not all who go to the Maharshi are intellectuals. All sincere devotees enjoy his grace. Sometimes philosophers have gone there and drifted away and simple folk with love in their heart have remained. Here, though never in the material world, the saying is made good 'to each according to his needs'. You can expect such devotees to tell you why they go there only when the lover can tell why he loves and the penitent why he worships.

# II

# Dr. Hafiz Syed

IT IS SAID and perhaps rightly too, that over this distracted world there is a greater sway of materialism than of spirituality. The majority of people are deeply sunk in materialism and therefore, have no inclination or desire to turn their attention towards spiritual values.

The rapid advancement of science with its wonderful achievements in the form of numerous discoveries and inventions, has added to the materialistic tendencies of mankind today.

The people in this modern age demand direct proof for everything they are told to believe in. They are not satisfied with mere assertions. As spiritual values can not be demonstrated in the same manner as material things are, people do not give even a moment's thought to the possibility of values, other than material which they see all round themselves. This sphere of spiritual and material values is based on two different angles. To quote a Tibetan Scripture, "The Self of matter and the Self of spirit cannot remain together, one of the twain must go!"

The reality of spiritual life cannot possibly be undervalued or ignored simply because the majority of people are drawn towards materialism. But for the glory and achievements of spiritual life, human civilisation would not have progressed nor could humanity have taken a step forward in the scale of evolution. The history of human civilisation has revealed, to no small extent, that solitary spiritual men have achieved great things and have rendered no small service in raising the standard of human life from animality to humanity and from humanity to divinity. The all-embracing influence of divinely inspired prophets and sages in all ages is still being felt in various parts of the world, and the fact that materialism has been unsettling our minds, and in spite of the alienation of our sympathy from and belief in higher values.

Of all countries, India has had the unique reputation of producing in its fold a larger number of saints and sages from time immemorial up to the present day. Every teacher of humanity has had his own way of dealing with his brethren. Some of them, say, for instance, Gautama the Buddha, Jesus Christ, Guru Nanak, Kabir and Sri Sankaracharya have gone about from place to place exhorting and admonishing the people of their times to live moral lives and shun the ways of falsehood and intrigue.

They used to give sermons to the eager crowds wherever they went and in this way drew a larger number of people to them, laid certain rules and regulations for everyday life, advised people to seek true happiness exempt from decay and to be helpful and charitable to each other. They thus laid the foundation of the various religions that are still in vogue in every part of the world.

Unlike all these saints, sages and prophets, Sri Ramana Maharshi's life and work tells quite a different tale. His way of serving mankind is in many ways unique and all his own. If we closely and critically survey his simple and evidently uneventful life from his earliest youth up to the present day, when he has completed what the Psalmists call three score years and ten, we find that he has never of his own accord desired or moved a finger to win people's attention towards him. Nor did he offer them any kind of spiritual or moral admonition to better their lives.

When the people of Tiruvannamalai discovered his presence at the foot of the Hill of Arunachala some of them were irresistibly drawn towards him and sought his help and guidance.

There has been a gradual evolution in his relation with the outside world. In his early days when he was observing complete silence, some approached him out of mere curiosity to see what the 'Brahmana Swami' looked like, while others were moved by an inner spiritual urge to visit him and receive his blessings. One person of the latter category was Sri Ganapathi Muni who had all the equipment necessary to understand, a being endowed with higher spiritual powers.

It is acknowledged on all sides that Sri Ganapathi Shastri was deeply learned in Hindu *shastras* and in the light of his knowledge given by the *rishis* of yore and having the requisite qualifications as laid down by the sacred scriptures, he knew full well how to appreciate a young sage. To his great joy, as we all know, he found that Sri Ramana Maharshi in his youth had acquired all the moral and spiritual qualities and had attained the highest spiritual enlightenment to which humanity ever aspires. It is he who made known to the outside world that the 'Brahmana Swami' was a great sage, whose spiritual eminence could not easily be gauged by an ordinary mortal.

One great quality which shone brilliantly in the Sage was that of complete desirelessness and a spirit of unreserved renunciation. The thought of the world with all its glaring trinkets never crossed his mind. He was deeply, unshakeably and permanently established in his highest Self that was full of bliss. Having found his rest and home in what he lovingly called, his 'father', he never cared to look at anything that the world prized highly.

Only recently (i.e. in the late1940s) he suffered from a sarcomatous growth on his arm, a disease which causes intense pain to the body. It was operated on thrice and the sage's serenity, poise and peace were not at all disturbed. He remained absolutely unmoved by the pain and suffering that is usually associated with such a condition. He firmly believed and teaches others in silence to understand that man is essentially a spiritual being, free from all change, decay, and death. He is not his body, nor his senses, nor even the mind.

They are all made of matter and therefore they are constantly moving and changing. It is this realisation that makes him truly happy, carefree, quiet and peaceful. Bhagavan Sri Ramana's life is the greatest proof of the reality of the spiritual life which is a challenge to materialism. He lived in his higher Self and is in constant communion with the supreme Reality.

Bhagavan's method of approach to Truth is all his own. He never dogmatises, he never sermonises, never gives any *mantram* or expects people to follow any set mode of worship.

What he does for us we cannot convey by word of mouth. His invisible gaze, silently, unobtrusively transforms the lives of the men and women who, by virtue of their past good deeds, are gathered around him, waiting for his benign attention and paternal guidance.

All his great work for the improvement and betterment of mankind is done invisibly and silently. His silence is more eloquent, more effective, more far-reaching than the sermons of any number of teachers put together. There is nothing wanting in him for us. His grace is ever ready for us. All that we have to do is to qualify ourselves by our self-effort and self- purification to make ourselves worthy of his attention.

The well known maxim, "God helps those who help themselves", holds good more in the case of his devotees than of others. We have to raise ourselves to his level of requirements.

Let a sceptic, an agnostic, or an unbeliever in higher values come to him with an open mind, with a genuine desire to understand what inner life is and to know what truth really means and it may be said without the least hesitation that his visit to Sri Bhagavan will never prove fruitless.

What the modern world wants is proof and demonstration. That proof is present in the life of this great sage of India who is in our midst to dispel the darkness of ignorance and restore the light eternal, which alone can grant us the peace and happiness that the world so badly needs.

# III

## Prof B.L. Atreya

A SAINT IS as great a necessity for human society as is a great scientist, a great thinker and a great leader, nay the necessity is even greater. For a scientist discovers the secrets of life and of the Universe, a thinker tries to understand the meaning and purpose of existence, and a leader tries to shape and transform humanity or a portion of it according to his own notions of what it ought to be.

A saint is one who makes a wholehearted effort to realise in himself, in his own life, the highest and furthest possibilities of human life, which in a natural course of evolution may take centuries to actualise.

A saint is a man perfected, a fulfilled hope of humanity, a successful experiment in human sublimation, and a source of inspiration and guidance to the travellers on the path to perfection. He is the embodiment of the highest values of humanity, an indubitable indication that ideals can be made real, that man can be what he ought to be, here and now.

His life is a measure of man's manhood, when it is lived in the midst of humanity and not in sanctified seclusion. It is a practical solution of the various puzzles of life, provided it is a comprehensive one. Considered from various points of view, a saint is the greatest asset to human society. A perfected being, he is the eternal beacon to *sadhakas* the world over.

I have read the biographies of many a saint, seen a number of them and have come in contact with some. I have had the privilege of being at the Ashram of Sri Ramana Maharshi for a short time in March 1940 and since then have been in correspondence with him.

He made a deep impression upon my mind, a mind that has been moulded by a study of scientific and philosophic writings of the east as well as of the west. The greatest peculiarity and merit of Sri Ramana Maharshi's life is that although he has moulded and perfected his personality on the lines of *Advaita Vedanta*, a purely Indian way of Self-realization, he is highly appreciated and resorted to by western seekers and by those Indians who have been educated on western lines.

One of the reasons for this fact may be that some English and French writers happened to praise him highly in their books. But the fact remains to be explained why these western seekers were themselves so well impressed by the Maharshi. Mere publicity does not in the least establish the greatness of saints, although it may make them known, as in the case of Jesus Christ, to a wider public.

Maharshi's greatness is more deeply founded. It is based on his actual living by the creed of *Advaita Vedanta* which holds that reality is one without a second, that everything in this Universe is but that reality which is Existence-Consciousness-Bliss.

True to his creed, he regards nothing as alien, none as other, no event as undesirable. For him the ideal is the real and the real is the ideal. He has no other relation with anyone but that of love. He thinks as much of others as he thinks of himself. Love, affection, kindness, mercy etc. which are expressions of one and the same thing, and the feeling of unity with all, ever flow from him. This is the secret of Maharshi's unique greatness and consequent popularity. The whole of humanity owes its homage to this great sage amidst us.

*Jnana* is like *akasha*. The supreme Self which is to be known through *sadhana* is also like the ether. The various objects we see in the world as well as the souls are like the ether. Therefore, who is to know which? What is to be known by what? The supreme realization is that there is no plurality. True knowledge is distinctionless. That knowledge is the Self, the light divine. That knowledge is Bhagavan Ramana.

May we offer our obeisance to this supreme Lord who came to save the world and who still abides and will ever abide with us in order to make us perfect.

May we, on this auspicious occasion, renew our faith in our Bhagavan and pay homage to him so that not only we, but the entire world may be saved.

# IV

## Anonymous

WITH THE INCREASE in distant visitors, the atmosphere at Ramanashram is growing more lively and Sri Maharshi often brings home a point by narrating stories from the past.

One day, last week, the photo of a piece of architecture at the Madurai temple was missing. A few minutes earlier, it had been seen by many people who had gathered in the hall but when Mr. Maurice Frydman wanted to see it, the photo could not be traced. The Maharshi asked some of the inmates what had become of it and the most surprising part of it was that the French lady who was stated to have obtained it was not herself aware of having done so.

Mr. Frydman utilised the occasion to ask a pointed question as to how this disappearance was viewed by the Maharshi himself.

The reply was, "Suppose you dream that you are taking me to Poland. You wake up and ask me, I dreamt so and so. Did you dream so or know it? And how do you view it?"

Frydman further asked, "But are you not aware of the happenings in front of you?"

Sri Maharshi replied, "These are all workings of the mind and the questions also."

Then Sri Maharshi narrated a story.

"When Sita was missed and Rama went about in search of her, Parvati was surprised and asked Siva, 'You had praised Rama as the perfect being. See how he behaves now and grieves at the loss of Sita.'

"Siva replied, 'If you are sceptical about Sri Rama's perfection then put him to the test. Transform yourself into Sita and appear before him.'

"Parvati did so and to her astonishment, Rama ignored her appearance and still cried. 'Ha Sita, Ha Sita', and moved like a blind man. Parvati was then convinced."

In the course of a conversation Dr. Henry Hand asked Maharshi, "Are you conscious of a brotherhood of invisible *rishis*?"

Sri Maharshi replied with a question, "If invisible, how to see them?"

Dr. Hand, "In consciousness".

Sri Maharshi continued, "In consciousness there is nothing external."

Dr. Hand asked, "Is there not individuality? I fear to lose my individual being."

Sri Maharshi, "Why fear to lose individuality? What is your state in dreamless sleep? Are you conscious of your individuality then?"

Dr. Hand, "It is possible."

Sri Maharshi, "But what is your experience? If the individuality be there would it be asleep?"

Dr. Hand, "That depends on the interpretation. What does Maharshi say?"

Sri Maharshi, "Maharshi does not speak for your experience. He does not force anything down your throat."

Dr. Hand, "I know. That is what I like so much about the Maharshi and his teachings."

Sri Maharshi, "Do you not really take great care to get sound sleep? Do you not prepare your bed carefully? And are you not anxious to lose your individuality in deep steep? Then why fear it?"

One visitor asked him, "How can one root out the sex idea?"

Sri Maharshi's reply was, "By rooting out the false idea of the body being the Self. There is no sex in the Self."

The visitor again asked, "How is one to realise it?"

Sri Maharshi said, "Because you think you are the body, you see another as the body. Difference in sex arises. But, you are not the body. Be the real Self and there is no sex."

# V

# Anonymous

IN 1943 (OR 1944), Dr. Jesudasan, known as Peria Annan (the Chinna Annan being Dr. Paton), accompanied by Dr. Raja went to Sri Ramanasramam. Peria Annan who was a highly qualified doctor and who had done his medical studies at Edinburgh, wanted to serve the poor. At the same time he had a deep spiritual longing, and spent long hours in prayer, meditation, and reading the scriptures. Some accused this odd *sanyasi* doctor of not giving his full attention to medical work and wasting his expert talents. He himself was disturbed about this seeming dichotomy in his life.

He went to Sri Ramanasramam and sat in silence before the Maharshi amidst several devotees. Solemn silence prevailed and after some fifteen minutes, Periannan ventured to speak out and seek Bhagavan's guidance. Smiling, the Maharshi said, "Some call me also a lazy fellow. Do what you feel like doing." Periannan realized in a flash that there was no real dichotomy in his life.

# VI

WHEN IN ANCIENT DAYS even Sri Dakshinamurti the Adi-guru, guru of all gurus was able to reveal the truth of that one Self only through silence, the speechless speech, who else can reveal it through speech?

In this connection, Sri Bhagavan once told the following story to Sri Muruganar. When the four aged Sanakadi *rishis* first saw the sixteen-year-old Sri Dakshinamurti sitting under the banyan tree, they were at once attracted by him, understanding him to be the real *Sadguru*.

They approached him, did three *pradakshinas* around him, prostrated before him, sat at his feet and began to ask very shrewd and pertinent questions about the nature of Reality and the means of attaining it. Because of the great compassion and fatherly love (*vatsalya*) which he felt for his aged disciples, the young Sri Dakshinamurti was overjoyed to see their earnestness, wisdom and maturity, and hence he gave apt replies to each of their questions.

As he answered each consecutive question, further doubts rose in their minds and still they asked further questions. Thus they continued to question Sri Dakshinamurti for one whole year, and he continued to clear their doubts through his compassionate answers.

Finally, however, Sri Dakshinamurti understood that if he gave more answers to their questions more doubts would rise in their minds and hence there would never be an end to their ignorance *(ajnana)*. Therefore, suppressing even the feeling of compassion and fatherly love which was welling up within him, he merged himself into the supreme silence. Because of their great maturity (which had been ripened to perfection through their year-long association with the *Sadguru*), as soon as Sri

Dakshinamurti thus merged himself, they too were automatically merged within, into silence, the state of Self.

Wonder-struck on hearing Sri Bhagavan narrating the story in this manner, Sri Muruganar remarked that in no book is it mentioned that Sri Dakshinamurti ever spoke anything. "But this is what actually happened" replied Sri Bhagavan.

From the authoritative way in which Sri Bhagavan thus replied and from the clear and descriptive way in which he had told the story, Sri Muruganar understood that Sri Bhagavan was none other than Sri Dakshinamurti himself.

# VII

*The author of this reminiscence is not known, but the events took place in 1935. Maurice Frydman eventually became a resident of Sri Ramanasramam for a period of nearly three years and during the later stages of his stay, he compiled "Maharshi's Gospel".*

ONE MORNING IN September, one Maurice Frydman, a consulting and electrical engineer announced himself before Sri Bhagavan. He entered the hall, hat in hand but with shoes still on. The Maharshi ordered a stool for him upon which he seated himself cross-legged for a short time and then he withdrew. After a wash and light refreshments he came back without shoes and squatted on the floor.

He stayed three days and was quite social and genial and friendly to everyone who responded similarly towards him. He tried to learn our ways and adapt himself to them. His clumsiness often evoked the good humoured laughter of the Maharshi who always put him right, as a father would a child.

He tried to learn from Maharshi something about realisation, raised doubts and had them cleared. Once he asked why there should be illusion if the individual soul is identical with the Supreme. Bhagavan gave him the usual answer (the answer is not given in the text) and then began to chew betel leaves. In the meantime, Mr.Frydman was ruminating and with dramatic gestures wanted to know why the ego should not be cut down at one stroke and destroyed so as to gain supreme bliss. The Maharshi stopped chewing his betel leaves long enough to smile, and then broke out into laughter and asked the questioner to hold out his ego so that the Maharshi could strike it down. Everyone in the hall laughed including Mr. Frydman and at the conclusion of the laughter Mr. Frydman addressed the Maharshi and said, "Yes, now I understand."

# VIII

## Varadachari

THOUGH I HAVE HAD unique opportunities of studying some of the characteristic works of Sri Ramana, yet it was only in April 1947 that I had the good fortune of beholding him face to face. This *darshan* of the sage is an experience in itself. It is not capable of being described. So very casual yet pregnant, so very unobtrusive yet deeply significant, almost everything that occurs in the Ashram seems to be inundated with the quiet consciousness of the Master. Such indeed was my reflective impression. Pleasant, deeply penetrating and inspiring somewhere in the depths, it showed that the activity of the spirit is of a different order and kind from what we know to be 'activity'.

# IX

## Maurice Frydman

JUST SIX MONTHS after I came to India, I was left alone and had no friends. The person whom I loved died and I had nothing to attract me in life.

Quite accidentally, just for fun, I dropped in at Tiruvannamalai. I went direct to the swami but I was ordered out by his disciples as I had not taken off my shoes.

After bathing and other preparations, I went again to the hall and remained there with the Maharshi for two hours.

Then I understood that I had met someone, the likes of whom I had never met before.

I did not then know what was meant by words like Maharshi and Bhagavan. I had no preconceived ideas and yet I felt that there was something extraordinary in that man.

I was told about his teachings but they were far too high for me. I did not understand what they meant but I felt a strong and lasting affection for him. I was alone in India and I attached myself to him just as a homeless dog would to his master.

Afterwards, whenever I felt worried, I used to go to Arunachala, and sit in his presence. In the early days I would be asking questions, but later when I began to visit him more and more, the discussion with him grew less and less.

Then I began to visit him almost every month. I knew no *sadhana* or *dhyana*. I would simply sit in his presence. To my questions, Sri Maharshi would say: "Find out who you are." I could not make out anything but all the same I felt happy.

Slowly some change came in me. Just as the egg grows and hatches only with the aid of the warmth of the mother I was also getting into shape slowly and steadily in his presence.

My mind became more quiet than before. Previously it was unhappy and never satisfied. Now a kind of security and peace began to be felt spontaneously.

I felt that Sri Maharshi was coming nearer and nearer as time passed. Afterwards I used to think of him whenever I felt unhappy. He used to appear before me and ask if I have not committed any sin. If I had erred or sinned, he used to hide himself for a time but later on appear and reply.

His affection was always there and as fire melts ice so his affection made my worries melt.

# X

## Swami Madhavananda

ON ONE OCCASION, probably in 1939, Sri P.M.N. Swamy, a staunch devotee of Bhagavan and secretary of Sri Ramana Satchidananda Mandali, Matunga, went to the Ashram at Tiruvannamalai to have *darshan* of Bhagavan and stayed for the day there with his wife and nine month old child, Ramanan.

They had their breakfast in the common dining hall in the morning. After finishing they went to wash their hands at the tap outside, leaving the child in the hall. By this time Ramanan crawled away somewhere and could not be seen. The perturbed father called out to the child as 'Ramana, Ramana'.

Bhagavan, who was then passing on his way to the meditation hall immediately responded to the call and the child also was found near the well in the Ashram compound. The response from Bhagavan naturally created a little puzzle in Sri

P.M.N. Swamy's mind because he thought that the call 'Ramana, Ramana' intended for his child might have been wrongly interpreted by Bhagavan.

Bhagavan was quick to read Sri Swamy's mind and told him, "Why do you feel puzzled when I responded to the call? Is there any difference between this Ramana (meaning himself) and that Ramana (meaning the child)?"

# XI

## K. R. K. Murthy

AN OLD WOMAN bent double with age used to go round and round Sri Bhagavan's hall and finally go near Bhagavan's seat and loudly sing songs composed extempore by her. Her spontaneous compositions used to pour forth effortlessly from her extremely devoted heart. She was not a learned lady, there night be some grammatical mistakes and errors in rhyme, rhythm, etc. She used to thus sing her prayers daily for obtaining the grace of Bhagavan.

One day Sri Bhagavan smilingly remarked that her songs seemed to be much better than those of her son. Her son was a scholar and from an ordinary point of view, the scholar's compositions ought to be superior but for Bhagavan those arising from the bottom of the heart with great devotion and emotion are more pleasing. Are not the standards of judgement different?

Whenever Bhagavan's physical body appeared to suffer from some ailment, some devotees used to prescribe medicines for relief, forgetting that Sri Bhagavan himself was *Vaidyanatha* who can cure all ills if he so willed. Sri Bhagavan used to take or apply the medicines just for the satisfaction of the devotees who prescribed the same and not for curing himself. He never wanted to wound the feelings of even the humblest devotees and he used to accept the medicines, though there was no necessity for any of them as far as he was concerned. Though the act is the same, the object is different.

One lady devotee was one day expressing to Bhagavan that she had come that day from a long distance. Bhagavan suddenly remarked, "You did not come. The train brought you here." The other side of the picture is more real to Bhagavan. She did not come there perhaps by her individual exertion but was brought by Bhagavan's grace.

In the early stages, Sri Ramanashramam was a lonely cottage in the burial ground. As the number of devotees frequenting the Ashram was increasing, so also was the joy of the thieves in the neighbourhood at the prospect of getting easy money from the Ashram.

They waited for an opportunity and one day suddenly broke into the Ashram at the dead of night. They freely used their sticks on every one of the inmates including Bhagavan. They enraged the devotees who were preparing to pay them in the same coin. Sri Bhagavan who was unmoved pointed out that, "*sahanam* was *sadhu dharma*", and that they should patiently bear with the thieves.

"We should not swerve from the path of our *dharma* irrespective of the acts or behaviour of evil doers, further it is not wise to knock down the teeth that bit the tongue", he said.

These words disarmed the devotees, who kept quiet while the thieves were busy. The thieves expected to go back with a fortune but with all their efforts could not secure more than ten rupees worth of valuables from the whole premises.

While the thieves were thus disappointed and dejected, Sri Bhagavan was reported to have suggested to them mercifully that they should take the food available in the kitchen. This sensational incident could not upset the peace of Bhagavan even for a while or make an impression on his mind (although it became the talk of the neighbouring town). The importance attached to this occurrence by the sage was nil.

Once Bhagavan, while passing through the hilly tracts inadvertently damaged a nest of wasps. The wasps furiously attacked the leg that pulled down their beloved home. Sri Bhagavan bore the unbearable pain patiently without offering the least resistance as his guilty leg which caused pain to them in his opinion, deserved the just punishment meted out to the same by the angry wasps. How different is Sri Bhagavan's reaction and his sense of justice which knows no fear or favour?

When a westerner invited the attention of Bhagavan to the poverty of the average Indian and his poorly furnished quarters, Sri Bhagavan replied that although the Indians did not possess many material comforts, they are not less happy on that account. As they do not feel the want of the same, they are able to enjoy life with what they have. How true and how correct! Happiness is not directly proportional to the material goods one possesses.

In Sri Ramanashram Sri Bhagavan used to occupy a sofa and many people used to think it was very comfortable and luxurious a seat for any person. Some used to remark why should a sage or *sanyasi* require such a seat, forgetting for the moment that Sri Bhagavan was accustomed to the roughest and hardest possible seats throughout his life and only towards the end he used the sofa to oblige certain devotees.

One day Sri Bhagavan was giving instructions to an attendant about binding the books for careful preservation. To supplement the instructions and show personally, he sat on the flat floor and remarked that it was very pleasant to sit on the ground. A high seat also was essential to enable a number of devotees to have *darshan* of Bhagavan simultaneously. Sri Bhagavan was accustomed to put up with anything which came his way and as he was not attached to any particular seat, he occupied the sofa for the convenience of the devotees. This was in spite of some physical discomfort in occupying that particular seat. Ordinary people think that the sofa is a nice seat. But Sri Bhagavan expressed at least once that the floor was much better. Are not the views different?

One day as usual Sri Bhagavan started for a walk towards Arunachala. On the way, there were some steps. While crossing over these Sri Bhagavan's leg slipped and was injured. Some devotees who noticed this examined the steps and found them to be uneven. Immediately some masons were called for and by the time they started work Sri Bhagavan returned to the spot and observed that they were cutting off some portions of the steps. "Why?" He questioned. "Why do you cut off the steps? The steps did nothing. It is only this leg that is at fault. Cut off the leg." How different is the saintly reaction!

# XII

## J. Suryaprakasa Rao

IN THE YEAR 1946, a friend of mine informed me about the glory of Tiruvannamalai and its sage. The photo of Bhagavan in a smiling posture was secured by me.

It was three years later during May 1949, that I decided to have his *darshan*. On entering into his presence, the general silence and serenity captivated me. At first I was partly anxious to get near to him and partly timid. I only mentally repeated, "Bhagavan I have come" as though it was a long expected meeting. He looked into my eyes. Even from the distance I could not stand the brilliance of those eyes. I tried to meditate. Presently there was some conversation. A European lady sat there attired in Indian style. After a repeated jingling of her bangles, Bhagavan asked in Telugu smilingly, "What is the matter?" Somebody replied, "She wore bangles", "Oh I see", said Bhagavan. He was then looking at some of the correspondence, at the playing of the squirrels, and at the feeding of the white peacock.

In the afternoon, by the time we came, the sitting had already commenced. There was no interruption to the supreme silence. A cultured family of a mother, husband and wife came and offered some tiffin which he took, washed his hands and resumed his inimitable posture. We sat still in silence for some time and took leave after prostrating to Sri Ramana Bhagavan.

# XIII

## K. K. Nambiar

PEOPLE WHO VISITED Sri Bhagavan during his life time, could not have failed to observe the characteristic pose in which he reclined on his sofa with eyes closed and his head supported with his left arm, particularly at the time of *Vedaparayana* and so on.

Some of us devotees sitting around used to watch him intently during such periods. On several occasions I used to mentally pray to him that on reopening his eyes, he should bestow a look at me and I must say I was never disappointed. So, it was crystal clear to me that prayers to Bhagavan need not be vocal and he felt, knew, and answered the inner prayers of all his devotees.

Conversely, there were also occasions when I sat at the feet of Sri Bhagavan and intently meditated on his form with closed eyes, and most often when I opened my eyes, Sri Bhagavan appeared to be watching me. It is a great comfort even now to recall the experience of those exquisite moments which stand out so vividly in my memory. Time hasn't effaced even a fraction of those vistas.

# XIV

## P.T. Muthuswami

MY JOY FOUND no limit when I had the *darshan* of Bhagavan Sri Ramana Maharshi on the 8th of June, 1947 at 9.20 a.m. Apart from Ashram inmates, Indians and foreigners, there used to be a stream of visitors both in the morning and the evening. Some visitors, with the permission of the Ashram authority, used to take snapshots of Bhagavan Sri Ramana Maharshi.

In my heart of hearts I was deeply thinking whether I could be so fortunate as to have a photo taken along with Sri Bhagavan. A good and pious idea indeed! But, the question of its fulfilment was entirely left to the entire grace of *guru dev*.

It so happened that a rich and a pious soul with a band of devotees from Andhra, came to the Arunachala temple and then to Sri Ramanasramam. They had the *darshan* of Sri Bhagavan in the morning and they arranged for a group photo to be taken along with him in the evening.

Sri Bhagavan stood in front of the small gate towards the eastern side, facing Arunachala Hill. Another devotee and myself were observing all this very keenly from a very respectful distance. One of the devotees seeing Sri Bhagavan standing, had very wisely brought a stool from the Ashram, upon which, *gurudev* sat. The photo was about to be taken when the *sarvadhikari*, in hurrying up to the spot, saw me and another devotee standing, and asked us to follow him. We both immediately followed him and joined the group photo. The photo was taken. My happiness was beyond expression. I have a copy of this eventful photo with me. This is how '*kripa*' of Bhagavan works miraculously.

Bhagavan can be compared to the *saptha rishis* of the ancient times. Those who came in contact with such a great personality, an embodiment of supreme Self-hood are really blessed. They should consider themselves very fortunate.

Those who lived at Sri Ramanashram knew full well how punctuality used to be observed in every activity of the Ashram. Even breakfast, lunch, tea and supper used to be served precisely at 7a.m., 11a.m., 3p.m., and 7.30p.m., respectively.

At the ringing of the bell, Sri Bhagavan would go to the dining hall from the main *darshan* hall. The devotees would follow him with great reverence. He used to sit in the middle of the dining hall and of all the devotees sitting in rows.

Different varieties of delicious dishes used to be served systematically and briskly by some of the devotees. Every variety, each in small quantity, used to be served to Bhagavan. He used to mix up the food, vegetables, chatnys and other things all into one paste and keep it ready.

When serving was finished Sri Bhagavan used to ask, "Finished?" meaning whether serving was completed. *Sarvadhikari* replying in the affirmative used to prostrate before him. Sri Bhagavan would then cast a benign glance all round and would nod his head signifying to commence eating. Perfect silence would be prevailing in the dining hall, although the number present would be more than a hundred. Sri Bhagavan would leave the plantain leaf after his meals, in such a clean manner, as it was placed, before meals were served. Not even a particle of rice would be left on it.

The very life of Sri Bhagavan was itself sacred scripture. He was moving *Veda* and *Upanishad*. His teachings were through silence. Who could have understood his immutable silence, the very nature of one's own Self!

# XV

## N. N. Rajan

BHAGAVAN SRI RAMANA is a guru to all those who have faith in him. He is a rare combination of *bhakti* and *jnana*. Some devotees feel that they are led through *jnana* towards Self-knowledge. Each individual is helped or taught by him either through silence or sometimes by words according to the needs of that person. Therefore, one is not aware what another gets by way of help from the guru and that becomes clear when the devotees compare notes of their experience.

Often Sri Bhagavan clears the doubts in the minds of the devotees even before they put questions to him. Devotees having some problems which they themselves could not solve come there with an ardent desire of asking Sri Bhagavan for a solution, but often, and to their amazement, they themselves find the solutions of the problems when they sit in his presence.

Such a method of teaching is nothing short of a miracle in its subtlest form. Miracles, as generally understood, are something spectacular and many persons are under the impression that the greatness of a saint or sage is directly proportionate to the number of miracles he performs. That way of thinking is not correct. Sri Bhagavan says that the greatest miracle is attainment of Self-knowledge and all other spectacular performances are of the world, hence illusory! He does not admit that he performs any miracles, but things do happen which we interpret in such a way.

In this connection, it would be interesting to narrate my experience. Once I met an old friend Mr. K. A. in Poona. In the course of our conversation, he told me that in 1919, he was informed by some devotees that a peacock and a cobra played with each other in Skandasram when Sri Bhagavan was residing there. To see this, he and a friend of his, decided to go there and verify what they had heard.

They arrived at Skandasram in the afternoon and sat there for a couple of hours hoping to see the bird and the snake, but they did not appear. They felt disappointed and returned home the same day with the belief that people circulate stories that are not correct. I too had heard about the story of the peacock and the snake at Skandasram, and I believed it because I had no cause to doubt the intention of those that told me about it. I tried to convince Mr. K.A., that miracles have no value to gauge the

greatness of a saint, which according to him have a value, and he
put forward very strong arguments to support his own case.

Mr. K. A. is a well-read old man, and the conversation
initiated a struggle in my mind whether to believe or discard as
untrue what I had heard. My mind was very uneasy for a couple
of days and it calmed down when it occurred to me that the
peacock and the snake could not have obliged Mr. K.A. and his
friend during the very short stay they made at Skandasram.

Sri Bhagavan's talks are very instructive and can be easily
understood by those who listen to him. He talks about his own
experience in very simple language. He generally speaks in Tamil,
Telugu or in Malayalam. He knows English but seldom speaks
in that language. People who do not know the Dravidian
languages ask questions in English and his replies are given in
Tamil which are then translated into English by an interpreter
for the benefit of the questioners. When he finds that the
translation is not correct he suggests appropriate English words
to the interpreter. He writes and composes in the three Indian
languages mentioned above and in Sanskrit too. Most of his
works have been translated into English and other languages.
From the study of such spiritual literature much benefit can be
derived, but one who is earnest in the quest of the Self, gets
abiding inspiration by personal contact with Sri Bhagavan. Since
he knows many languages, it is possible to converse with him
and get more benefit than from reading books alone.

I have had opportunities to talk to Sri Bhagavan and one
of them is mentioned here. One day I went to see Gurumurtham
and the garden near it. These two places are well known to those
who have read his biography. It is in this garden that Bhagavan's
uncle recognised him as his nephew Venkataraman, who had
left his home some three years earlier. After visiting the two

places I returned to the Ashram and told Sri Bhagavan that the place now is more or less an open ground and is not a garden as described by Sri Narasimhaswamy in his book *Self Realization*. Sri Bhagavan immediately began to describe how the garden was then and proceeded further to describe his life during his sojourn there. He said that he was taking shelter in a lamb pen which was hardly high enough for him to sit erect. If he wanted to stretch his body on the floor, most of it was out in the open. He wore only a *kaupina* and had no covering over the rest of his body. If it rained he remained on the wet and sodden ground where sometimes water stood a couple of inches deep! He did not feel any inconvenience because he had no 'body sense' to worry him. He felt that sunrise and sunset came in quick succession. Time and space did not exist for him! He then tried to describe the state of his awareness of the Self and his awareness of the body and things material. To him the sun of absolute Reality made the phenomenal world disappear and he was immersed in that light which dissolves diversity into the One without a second!

It is not possible to express exactly the thrill felt by all of us who were listening to him. We all did feel as if we were transported into that condition to attain that which we are striving for. There was a deep silence in the hall for some time during which everyone present felt peace and happiness. It occurred to me then that Bhagavan, while narrating any incident of his life, takes the opportunity to teach us, and I told him that when he spoke we felt as if it was easy to experience the Self and even as if we had glimpses of it. We asked him exactly how one has to proceed to be in that state of continuous awareness which he had described. Sri Bhagavan, with his sparkling eyes, looked at me benevolently, raised his hands and said,

"It is the easiest thing to obtain. The Self is always in you, around you and everywhere. It is the substratum and the support of everything. You are experiencing the Self and enjoying it every moment of your life. You are not aware of it because your mind is on things material and thus gets externalised through your senses. Hence you are unable to know it. Turn your mind away from material things which are the cause of desires, and the moment you withdraw your mind from them you become aware of the Self. Once you experience the Self, you are held by it, and you become 'That which is the One without a second.'"

When he finished his words I again felt in the same way as I felt on the first day I met him in 1923 — that Sri Bhagavan is a big power house and his power or grace overwhelms us, whatever our ideas may be and leads us into the channel flowing into the Self. It became clear to me that we can have the knowledge of the Self if only we take the path into which a realised person or guru directs us.

In conclusion I wish to say that one should constantly meditate that one is not the body or the mind. Unless the mind is in contact with the senses, we cannot get any report from our ears, eyes etc. We must therefore still the mind by disconnecting it from the senses and thus get beyond them to experience the Self. What we learn from sense perception is only relative knowledge. Knowledge of the Self can be learnt only by sitting at the feet of one who has realised it; what others tell you is mere talk. Bhagavan Sri Ramana is one of those Masters who has realised the Self and like all other Masters who preceded him, he helps us proceed rapidly to attain Self-knowledge.

# XVI

## Madhavi Ammal

*Srimathi Madhavi Ammal, a staunch devotee, was fortunate in having many opportunities to talk to Sri Bhagavan freely and appeal to him direct for upadesa. Sri Bhagavan made things easy for her in many ways, one of which was talking to her in her native Malayalam. He gave a patient hearing to her tales of woe which were many. This is visible in a film on Sri Bhagavan which is screened occasionally at the Ashram. The devotee seems to have almost wrested the upadesa from the Guru by her perseverance according to the following narrative of hers.*

I KNEW FULL well that Sri Bhagavan gave no formal *upadesa* (initiation) but I kept on asking for it whenever an opportunity presented itself. Invariably Sri Bhagavan used to reply, "Who is the Guru and who is the *sishya* (disciple)? They are not two. There is but One Reality. It is in you and It can neither be given nor taken. But you may read books for intellectual understanding."

On March 12, 1934 after prayers at the Shrine of Sri Mathrubhuteswara I went to the old hall. Only the attendant Madhava Swami was with Sri Bhagavan. When I made my usual request Sri Bhagavan laid aside the newspaper he was reading and sat in *padmasana*, quite absorbed. I then recited a (general) hymn of praise to the Guru in Telugu and also *Aksharamanamalai* in Telugu (the hymn on Sri Arunachala by Sri Bhagavan). Sri Bhagavan turned to Madhava Swami and said, "She has prayed to Sri Arunachala." This struck me as meaning that Sri

Arunachala will give the initiation and also that Sri Bhagavan and Sri Arunachala are not two. Sri Bhagavan resumed his state of absorption and I had my persistent request for *upadesa*. But he continued to sit motionless. Finally I begged of him, "Am I not a competent person to receive *upadesa?* Sri Bhagavan should himself tell me about this. Even if Sri Bhagavan confirms this how is it that I adopted him as my Guru immediately on hearing of him (she was just told that a Rishi lived at the foot of the Hill)? Will it all be in vain?" Immediately on my speaking thus I found a bright light emanating from Sri Bhagavan's holy face, and the effulgence filled the whole Hall. I could not see Sri Bhagavan's body but only the brilliance. I shed tears in profusion. The whole incident could have lasted just two seconds! I prostrated to Sri Bhagavan. There was a smile on his face but no movement otherwise. After a while Sri Bhagavan turned to me as if to ask, "Are you rid of your mania?" Yes, I was. He then took a piece of paper, wrote a *sloka* (verse) on it and gave it to me saying, "You can make use of it in meditation."

This is the *sloka:*

I adore Guha the Dweller in the Cave of the Heart, the Son of the Protector of the Universe, the Pure Light of Awareness beyond thought, the Wielder of the weapon of *Jnana Sakti* and the Remover of the ignorance of blemishless devotees.

And again he smiled graciously.

This was wonderful *upadesa* indeed by a Master rare to see. My Master taught me the great truth that there is only ONE. The proper Guru is one who shows what is. This was but a practical demonstration of the saying

"The Master's face reveals Brahman. You attain Brahman through Grace."

౧ ౨

# RECOLLECTIONS

## K.R.K. Murthy

WITH A VIEW to record Sri Bhagavan's voice and preserve the same for posterity, someone raised a discussion on the sound recording machines in the presence of Bhagavan. Sri Bhagavan agreed with what they said, regarding this wonderful machine. Seeing that Sri Bhagavan was very favourably disposed towards the same, they wanted to pursue the matter further and fix up a date for recording Sri Bhagavan's voice. At that moment Sri Bhagavan replied, "My real voice is silence; how can you record that?" In this connection he narrated the story of the saint Thandavaraya, who by his dynamic silence stilled the minds of several people, for three full days.

Once when someone was expressing that all sensations near his hip were not being felt for some time, Sri Bhagavan quickly remarked, "How nice will it be if the whole body becomes like that? We will be unaware of the body."

One attendant of Bhagavan was reading to Bhagavan in the night. The attendant heard snoring sounds and stopped reading thinking that Bhagavan was asleep. Immediately Bhagavan questioned him as to why he stopped. Again the attendant continued and similar snoring sounds proceeding from Bhagavan made him stop again. But Sri Bhagavan was quite alert and asked him to continue. Is it not a job to find out when Bhagavan is inattentive?

Once Sri Bhagavan said, "If you remain quiet you do the greatest service. One who is abiding in *Atma nishtai* is always doing greater service (*sishrusha*) to the guru, than one who does some service physically." Guru is one who shows the way to *Atma nishtai* (abidance in the Self) and the disciple is one who follows.

"If one wants to commit suicide, even a small implement or knife is sufficient. For murdering others, bigger ones are required. Similarly for oneself, one or two words are sufficient but to convince others, books after books have to be written."

"This Ashram is a place where people can stay and improve and not remark or criticise. In the beginning people come here with the best of intentions to secure the grace of the swami. After a time, they begin to comment, 'This is not right, that is not right', and engage themselves in some kind of activity and run after power and position and, as it were, forget for what they have come here."

"Always it is safer to use cheap and ordinary items as no one then cares to cast a greedy eye upon them."

"One who does the work without the feeling of doer-ship escapes misery and unhappiness; work then becomes more a pleasure and not exacting."

— *Sri Bhagavan*

ॐ

# OUR NATURAL STATE

## A 'Pilgrim'

*The author of this article is unknown but the incident must have taken place some time after 1946 when the answer to D.S. Sarma's question was first printed. The quotation was first printed in* Vedanta Kesari *in January 1947 (Vol. 33, No. 9, P. 327)*

I WAS ON MY long cherished pilgrimage to Bhagavan Sri Ramana. On the train I was chewing the cud of doubt. In the December and January issues of the *Vedanta Kesari*, I had read the answer Maharshi gave to the question put to him by Prof. D.S. Sarma as to whether there was a *sadhana* period in the life of Sri Bhagavan previous to his enlightenment. Sri Dilip Kumar Roy had put the answer in a poetical garb under the caption, "My yoga" and Prof. Sarma had given his question and Maharshi's answer under the title, *'Sahajasthithi'*. I reproduce below the answer of Sri Bhagavan,

"I know no such period of *sadhana*. I never performed any *pranayama* or *japa*. I know no *mantras*. I had no rules of meditation or contemplation. *Sadhana* implies an object to be gained and the means of gaining it. What is there to be gained which we do not already possess? In meditation, concentration and contemplation what we have to do is only not think of anything but to be still. Then we shall be in our natural state."

This indeed was an intriguing situation for me. I had read in the *Life and Teachings of Sri Ramana* of the severe *sadhana* he did in the lonely rooms of the big temple at Tiruvannamalai and in the caves on the hill. Now here is Bhagavan himself denying it all! And more than that, how can illumination come without *sadhana*? That was something against the word of the scriptures. However, I consoled myself with the thought that at the Ashram, I might have the chance of placing my difficulties before Sri Maharshi himself.

It was one of those beautiful mornings in Tiruvannamalai. After my daily ablutions and duties I was ready for the *darshan* of Bhagavan. As I approached the Maharshi's room I could feel the peace that was radiating from his room. I entered the room and then came my first shock. I expected to see something glorious, a face surrounded by a halo, etc. I didn't find any of these. Has he not said, I was reminded, in his answer that Self-realisation does not mean that something would descend upon us as something glorious? Has he not said, "People seem to think that by practising some elaborate *sadhana* the Self would one day descend upon them as something very big and with tremendous glory and they would then have what is called *sakshatkaram*."

None of the biographies state that Bhagavan did any *sadhana* after coming to Tiruvannamalai. I might have interpreted Bhagavan's period of silence and solitude as a period of *sadhana*, although it has been clearly stated both by Bhagavan and the writers who have written about him, that no *sadhana* was taking place during this period.

That winning smile that accompanied his greeting me meant more than Self-realisation. He beckoned to me to sit down and I sat there for more than two hours not knowing the passage of time. I realised then that silence is more eloquent than words. I dared not break the silence to raise my own petty doubts.

Later, though, I communicated my wish to place my doubts before the Maharshi and the consent came by midday.

When we reassembled before Sri Bhagavan at three, I was given the typescript of the question and answer to read and I read it aloud. I had framed my question thus:

**Question:** "You have said here that you know no such period of *sadhana;* you never performed *japa* or chanted any *mantra;* you were in your natural state. I have not done any *sadhana* worth the name. Can I say that I am in my natural state? But my natural state is so different from yours. Does that mean that the natural state of ordinary persons and realised persons are different?"

**Answer:** "What you think to be your natural state is your unnatural state. (And this was my second shock that shook me from the slumber of my pet notions). With your intellect and imagination you have constructed the castles of your pet notions and desires. But do you know who has built up these castles, who is the culprit, the real owner? The 'I' who really owns them and the 'I' of your conception are quite different. Is it necessary that you put forth some effort to come into the 'I' who owns these, the 'I' behind all states?"

"Would you have to walk any distance to walk into the 'I' that is always you? This is what I mean by saying that no *sadhana* is required for Self-realisation. All that is required is to refrain from doing anything, by remaining still and being simply what one really is. You have only to dehypnotise yourself of your unnatural state. Then you have asked whether there is any difference between the natural state of ordinary persons and realised persons. What have they realised? They can realise only what is real in them. What is real in them is real in you also. So where is the difference?"

"Even then, some may ask", the Maharshi continued, reminding me so vividly of those *Upanishadic rishis*, "where is the conviction that one's Self is *sakshat* all right, that no *sadhana* is required at all for Self-realisation? Well, do you need anybody to come and convince you that you are seated before me and talking to me? You know for certain that you are seated here and talking to me."

"When we read a book, for instance, we read the letters on the page. But can we say that we are reading only the letters? Without the page of the book where are the letters. Again we say that we are seeing the picture projected on a canvas. No doubt we are seeing the picture, but without the canvas where is the picture?"

"You can doubt and question everything but how can you doubt the 'I' that questions everything. That 'I' is your natural state. Would you have to labour or do *sadhana* to come into this natural state?"

റ്റ ൗ

# A SPIRITUAL TORCH

## Paul Brunton

THE WORLD SELDOM recognises a prophet at his true worth during his own lifetime, but the Maharshi has been more fortunate. His repute has begun to ripple out and is destined to go right around the world.

He has made it possible for us to understand what seems to exist today only as a mere echo of the words of the great spiritual teachers of former ages; the blessed *nirvana* of Buddha, the kingdom of heaven of Jesus, the liberation of Sri Krishna, and the supreme good of the early philosophers.

The Maharshi enjoys that divine condition and demonstrates in his own person this unique attainment. While metaphysicians argue vainly about the reality of our world, scientists throw wet blankets around the ardours of religionists and the average man meekly looks on; this serene Sage knows the eternal reality, experiences the everlasting bliss and expresses the highest Truth in his teachings. Withal, he radiates these things to every sensitive person who comes within his orbit and to every humble and teachable soul entering his sanctified presence.

His doctrine is as old as the Hill of Arunachala itself, yet, being self-found as the result of his own overwhelming spiritual illumination and not as the result of studying other men's books, it comes to us as fresh in presentation as the latest words of the pundits of western science.

If you can plumb the mind's depths, he teaches, you will eventually arrive at a point where both the thinking intellect and personal self seem to disappear, becoming reabsorbed by the hidden element out of which they were created. That element is none other than the absolute Being, the partless Reality, the one Self underlying, the birth and death of mortal men and material worlds.

The Maharshi's practical course of effort for discovering this reality is extremely simple, so simple, that our modern over-active minds may turn away unsatisfied and seek complicated elaborate yoga disciplines and yet it is extremely subtle. It is as effective for the devotional type of person as for the intellectual.

Set up a mental current of self-questioning, teaches the sage, attempt to ferret out what you really are, and to trace the living being who thinks and feels within your body. Watch your thoughts in the process and then endeavour to pin them down to the stillness out of which they arise. If you persist and apply yourself to frequent meditation on this topic, you will ultimately track thought to its origin, Self to its lair and consciousness to its primal partless state.

The personal sense of 'I' will collapse and disappear, being replaced by the impersonal sense of That, the absolute spirit which breathes life into us all, which not only maintains the existence of your mind and body but also the minds and bodies of all creatures.

This technique of Self-enquiry is really more simple than the ancient systems of yoga, and should therefore be easy to practise. Because of its subtle nature, however, and of our numerous tendencies towards excessive mental and material activity, it becomes difficult. The most effective way of overcoming that difficulty which I know and of which the ancient *Upanishads* often remind us, is to seek out the society of the Brahman-knowers, the spiritually illumined, and to sit at their feet, as the same texts poetically put it.

The Maharshi, in his modesty, will hardly ever refer to this fact, but those of us who have basked in his spiritual sunshine have found the way to the spirit made easier. For he continually broadcasts telepathically the divine atmosphere which has now become his very nature. In effect, he mysteriously communicates his spiritual calm to our troubled souls.

This investigator of the soul's domain has solved stubborn questions which have puzzled the thinkers amongst men since reason first evolved. Western scientific psychology is heading straight for the explanation which he gives of that apparent mixture of beast and angel called man. The Maharshi's method of psychoanalysis is far removed from the queer, muddled method of Freud, whose materialistic and sexual emphasis caused him to miss the divine.

The reward which waits for those who practise the technique advocated by the Maharshi is nothing less than nirvana itself, at the most, and mental tranquillity at the least. Those who think that the *nirvana* of the sage is a kind of never ending boredom should spend a few months in his society. The experience will correct their mistake and make good their ignorance.

When I first travelled around India interviewing her holy and learned men, I was amused to note how their numerous theories and explanations contradicted each other. The trouble was that the dust of so many generations has gathered upon the sacred texts and scholarly books that the real meaning of these volumes has been overlaid.

Scarcely one of those who granted me audience could speak from personal experience, and most could only quote the opinions of others. But the Maharshi's teachings flow out of his own original teachings, realization of Truth, and to that extent he stands solitary as the peak of Arunachala itself. He illustrates perfectly those words of the great yogi, Patanjali, 'The seer abides within himself, for he ever dwells within that sacred centre wherein God speaks to man'.

Even while I write, a grey squirrel hops into the Ashram hall, plays purposelessly for a while, and then squats contentedly under the Maharshi's divan. You are as safe there, brother squirrel, as on your own sheltering tree, for the sage's attitude towards you is no different from your Creator's. There is nothing but love in his heart towards all creatures and even if, perchance you were to bite him, he would not hit you in return.

Since that day when I first found him, absorbed in the mysterious trance of *samadhi*, I have travelled in many lands but always my thoughts turned towards Tiruvannamalai as the Muhammedan turns his face during prayer towards Mecca. I knew that somewhere in the wilderness of this world there was a sacred place for me. Since that day, it has become a sacred place for many others who have never left Europe and America. For at the sage's feet, I picked up a spiritual torch and carried it to waiting souls in the lands of the west. They welcomed the light with eagerness. There should be no virtue to be accredited to me for that, for whatsoever benefit has accrued to Western seekers comes from the torch which was lit by the Maharshi himself. I was only the unimportant "link boy", the humble carrier. And now that I have returned to the ever luring Hill of the Holy Beacon, I pray the gods of destiny that they may keep the captive here for many years.

# BHAGAVAN TREATED FOR ECZEMA

## T.K.S.

SOMEWHERE ABOUT 1935 a doctor friend of mine visited the Ashram and stayed with Bhagavan for over six weeks. He was deeply pious and devoted to Sri Ramanuja Sampradaya. His devotion to Bhagavan Sri Ramana Maharshi was equally great. He was a great congress worker. I remember that he was a good friend of Swamy Ramananda of Hyderabad, for I saw him in his company, when the Swamiji visited Bhagavan at the time of the Government of India's police action against the Nizam's State. Later this doctor himself became a minister of the state and was in charge of the finance portfolio.

The doctor's visit synchronised with the occasion when Bhagavan had an attack of eczema for which he was being treated by the local doctors. This doctor being more qualified than others took the lead in treating Bhagavan. The treatment went on for about a fortnight. Patches of white ointment were seen all over Bhagavan's body. After a fortnight, the disease seemed to get under control. The doctor was happy and congratulated himself that he had the opportunity to treat Bhagavan with success.

Lo! His elation was short lived. The disease burst out again with redoubled vigour. The doctor said to me that it was a lesson to him to curb his ego and continued the treatment with great humility and prayerfulness, praying to Bhagavan that he must effect the cure himself and that he (the doctor) was but his instrument.

The divine patient now seemed to make steady progress and gave consolation to the doctor that his prayer was being heard. The doctor oscillated between elation and curbing of his ego according to the disease as it decreased or increased. All along this course of treatment and from the time the doctor friend arrived at the Ashram, I had the pleasure of his acquaintance and of talking to him about Bhagavan. We used to sit until late in the night and talk and talk about Bhagavan, so absorbed in our conversation that we had no sense of space or time.

It was the month of December and Bhagavan's *jayanthi* was arriving. I used to talk to my doctor friend about the speciality of *jayanthi darshan,* for on the *jayanthi* day Bhagavan had a special glow of light about him and his starry eyes shed a special lustre and those around experienced the ambrosia or the elixir of life. It is for experiencing this light or bliss of being that devotees flocked to him from near and far. Though this experience was obtained on normal days too, it was very intense on particular occasions like *jayanthi, Mahapooja* and *Karthikai* days, as also it was when great souls met him.

It is of this special favour to devotees that I was telling my doctor friend. I used to call it the special grace of Bhagavan on the *jayanthi* occasion.

It was at this time that Bhagavan was putting the eczema ointment over his body. What could be the nature of this *jayanthi* dream? This was the anxiety of my doctor friend and he used to ask me often, "Mr. Iyer, how will Bhagavan give special *darshan* to his devotees with these white paints and patches on him? I am sorry that I shall not have the fortune of having it. Why should he have this disease at this time when I am visiting him?"

I used to reply, "Wait and see if he will be Bhagavan your patient, or the Bhagavan of my description dispensing special grace on the *jayanthi* occasion."

The *jayanthi* day came. There were the usual decorations, gathering of devotees, *pujas*, music etc. Bhagavan was seated in a specially decorated *pandal.* All the same he was to my doctor friend still his patient Bhagavan and not the Bhagavan of my description. I was not sorry that Bhagavan was going to belie my expectation and that of other devotees who were accustomed to have the *jayanthi* gift of Bhagavan. (They used to call it Bhagavan's *jayanthi* gift). I was only sorry for my doctor friend.

It was 9 a.m. on the *jayanthi* morning. All eyes were riveted on Bhagavan. There were the longing prayers of the souls gathered around Bhagavan. Suddenly there appeared the special features of Bhagavan on his face and eyes. The *nija mouna bhava*, its fullness expressing itself as *Atma Rama - Muditha vadana* and Dakshinamurthi. The Bliss of his Being ebbing over his countenance beautifying it, true to the words of Dakshinamuthi's names: *Sundara, Sundara, Sundara,* I am the perfection of beauty of the inner Self. I am 'I'. *Ahamevaham.*

The peace of his Being permeated the atmosphere and all those that were gathered around, keeping them enthralled in the grace that was his. The peace that passeth all understanding. The unborn (*Ajayamana*) was revealing himself through a form. Bhagavan was Bhagavan telling us without telling *Tat Twam Asi* (That Thou art).

"*Tat Twam Asi, Tat Twam Asi*" nithyam.

I whispered to my doctor friend to tell me if Bhagavan was his patient Bhagavan or *Jayanthi* Ramana Bhagavan. He could only nod his head in acceptance of my remarks. He was all spellbound and in wonder. He remarked later, "Mr. Sundaresh, I have lived to see this great marvel. Who would say he is like any of us? Yet he condescends to be one of us and that is our great fortune. My patient is my darling and God."

ങ ൝

# SRI RAMANA

## Major A.W. Chadwick (Sadhu Arunachala)

*The author was a well-known and ardent devotee
of Sri Bhagavan, who stayed at the Ashram for over a
quarter of a century without any thought of return to
England. He used to spend many hours in meditation
adhering strictly to a regular time-table. He was a model
of steadfast sadhana which he kept up after Bhagavan's
Mahasamadhi till the end of his life in 1962.*

RAMANA MAHARSHI WAS UNIQUE in that he was an
out and out *advaitin*. There were no half-measures with
him. Now to be an *advaitin* of this description is extremely
difficult. While for most of us, it is all intellectual gymnastics,
for him it was his life. At the early age of sixteen he had realized
the Self, and had never swerved from it or come down to a
lower function ever after. When he was asked about his
movements in the temple and his period of *mounam,* if his
state had not become more stabilized as a result of this *sadhana*
he emphatically stated that, "No change had occurred, nothing
new since then had ever happened. It's the same now as then."

But for himself he saw nothing wonderful in it. It was the
natural state and it was really strange that others should find
any difficulty in realising or being it themselves. "You are the

Self", he repeatedly said, "nothing but the Self. How can you be anything else? There are not and cannot be two selves, one to know the other. Just be yourself!"

Put like this, of course, it sounds easy but experience teaches us another tale. Every word is true, but *vasanas* are so persistent and desires of such long standing that they get in the way and prevent the pure vision. Habits are deep within us and refuse to be rooted out.

Countless are the number of existences lived in the past with which we have been associated. Just to sit quiet and forget them even for a moment seems impossible. Rather does it seem to cause those long forgotten existences to bubble up and fill the mind with their inanities.

Yet sitting in his presence the thing became so transparent that one was convinced for the time being, that all troubles were ended, and one was forced back on oneself in spite of all obstacles. And this was the wonder of his presence.

It was not in the few words he set on paper or the verbal instructions he gave to sincere enquirers that his real teaching lay but in his silent presence. Then questions would drop away unasked, difficulties of meditation vanished and the mind became still. It was unbelievable how easy it suddenly became.

Not only the effect of his presence but the shining example of himself, left indelible marks on those who had the good fortune to spend some time with him. There was no use in saying it could not be done. Here was one who had done it. One might tell oneself that the state could be nothing but one of blankness and convince oneself that it was not to be desired but here was he, exhaling bliss which overflowed out of its superabundance to even the meanest of us sitting there with him. It was marvellous! Was there ever another like him? What silent power! And what a fountain of hope!

# Sri Bhagavan and the Mother's temple

## Major A.W. Chadwick (Sadhu Arunachala)

BHAGAVAN WAS DEEPLY interested in the construction of the shrine built over his mother's samadhi. He attended every function in connection with it, placing his hands in blessing on the various objects that were to be enclosed in the walls. At night, when no one was about, he would walk round and round the construction consecrating it. That he should take such a demonstrative part in anything has a very deep significance. It was extremely rare and has been doubted by many, but I myself was an eye-witness to these things and can vouch for their truth.

He took a personal interest in the cutting of the Sri *Chakra Meru* in granite (pyramidal form), which was installed in the completed temple and is regularly worshipped. This is about one and a half feet square and proportionately high. At the time of the *kumbabhishekam* on the penultimate night before the sacred water was poured over the images, he personally supervised the installation in the inner shrine. It was an extremely hot night and with three charcoal retorts for melting the cement adding to the heat. It must have been intolerable inside the airless cave of the inner shrine. Yet for approximately one and a half hours Bhagavan sat there telling the workmen what to do.

On the last night of the function he went in procession, opening the doors of the new hall and temple and passing straight up into the inner shrine, where he stood for some five minutes with both hands laid on the *Sri Chakra* in blessing. I happened that night to be at his side the whole time. This was unusual, as I deliberately avoided taking a prominent part in such things, preferring to watch from the back.

Strangely, something made me keep by him on this occasion and on account of this I was able to understand his deep interest in the temple and especially in the *Sri Chakra*. It was because of this knowledge that I was instrumental, after Bhagavan's passing, in persuading the Ashram authorities to institute the *Sri Chakra pujas* six times a month.

The explanation for this unusual action on Bhagavan's part may be found in the necessity of Siva always to be accompanied by Shakti. The world would stop otherwise. On the only occasion when such a *puja* was performed, shortly after the dedication of the temple during the life of Bhagavan, he refused to go for his evening meal, but insisted on remaining a witness of it until the end. Someone remarked how magnificent it had been and that it would be a good thing if such *pujas* could be performed regularly, "Yes, but who will take the trouble?" asked Bhagavan. Trouble is being taken now and it undoubtedly has the blessings of Bhagavan.

CS 80

# THE IMMUTABLE ATMOSPHERE

## N. O. Mehta

DILIP KUMAR ROY and myself reached Tiruvannamalai at about 7 p.m., 17th February 1949 after a tiresome and dusty journey. Our discerning hostess, a Parsi lady, was rightly more concerned about our having the *darshan* of Bhagavan, as the Maharshi is universally called there, and consequently we promptly went to the prayer hall.

To our pleasant surprise we found Tiruvannamalai a substantial town with good roads, and electric lighting. The Ashram is one and a half miles beyond the town, just at the foot of the beautiful Arunachala Hill, so sacred and so powerfully evoked in some of the wonderful verses written by the Maharshi years ago. The prayer hall is a nice, clean, fair sized building which could perhaps accommodate 100 to 150 people without difficulty. We went into the hall, but either by habit or by some sort of inhibition or training, we did not prostrate ourselves in the traditional fashion. We only made a deep bow and took our seats. The critical eye noticed the scrupulous cleanliness of the hall, the intensely devout mien of the people and the utter simplicity and grandeur of the entire atmosphere.

Bhagavan himself, lean, of medium height, wheat complexioned, was reclining on a sofa surrounded by a low, folding wooden barrier to keep the fervent worshippers from touching his body. It is on this sofa that the Maharshi spends his time either sitting or reclining whether by day or by night. Close to the couch is an incense burner, which is going on all the time. There is one more burner with incense sticks at the foot of the couch. The purifying fumes are always rising in the air. Sometimes the Maharshi himself is stocking the burner and putting in more and more incense in the bowl. Just on the side of the couch is a high stool with a time piece, a table lamp and a few bottles of medicine. In front of the sofa is a small book case with a few books in English and in Tamil, principally of the Maharshi's own writing. I counted five wall calendars hung at the odd corners including one containing a portrait of Jawaharlal Nehru.

People were squatting cross legged, some with eyes shut, some eagerly looking at Bhagavan, but all absolutely silent. People were coming in and going out after doing the prostration. All this homage left the Maharshi untouched, or was it only my illusion, for those wonderful eyes seemed to take in everything even though they had a faraway, distant look.

Prayers from the *Upanishads* were being recited by three young disciples. I felt the magnificent rhythm of the Sanskrit language more powerfully than I have ever felt it before. I immediately realized how the great *mantras* and the verses of the *Vedas* and the *Upanishads* must have sounded in a bygone age at the morning and evening prayers in forest hermitages. The recitation was wonderful, the intonation accomplished and egoless. One was immediately hushed to devout silence. The prayers were wound up with the invocation to Bhagavan Ramana himself.

How is one to describe the atmosphere? 1 have referred to the trifles because though they attracted my attention on the first evening, they ceased to have any significance the very next morning. All that I felt was, that I was face to face with a Reality which transcended all that I had dreamt of him. Here was a great sage whose *darshan* was undoubtedly a privilege. I instinctively felt that here was India at its highest, for here was the deepest realization of the Reality transcending all mundane factors and bringing peace which passes all understanding. Let me, however, get along with trifles, for even they may have some usefulness.

At 7.30 p.m. was the evening meal and some thirty to forty people sat down to a simple meal, irrespective of race or rank, with the Maharshi occupying a corner. Rice and curry are served, some pulses and sometimes little vegetable delicacies on a plantain leaf. The Maharshi is the most careful diner of all, for he leaves no particle of surplus food on his platter. Food is served to all servants and masters by the very people who render service to the Maharshi, the same who look after the Ashram and who chant those wonderful verses from the *Vedas* and the *Upanishads* at the morning and evening prayers. Here was truly the hermitage of a saint where nothing mattered but an unceasing effort to know and feel the eternal Brahman.

The Maharshi finishes his meal quietly and slowly, but the diners leave the hall as they please, and so far as the Maharshi's presence for the day is concerned, it is all over with the completion of the evening meal. There is a radio set in a corner of the prayer hall. The Maharshi is interested in everything including the feeding of monkeys, peacocks and squirrels.

After the meal we left the Ashram to go to our accommodation across the road. There are some charming little cottages, which have been built by the people who have been regularly coming to have the *darshan* of Bhagavan and with some luck one can have one of these cottages. However, the creature comforts to which we were used no longer mattered. We were in a world totally different from the one we had left behind. The values were also different and all that was important now was to get up in time for the morning prayers at 4 a.m.

It is difficult to reproduce the atmosphere of the morning prayers. The lights are still on. The Maharshi is holding his hands over the incense burner, the disciples chant the *Vedic* prayer in a firm and resonant voice. The stately rhythm of these prayers creates an amazing atmosphere of peace and sanctity. For more than forty minutes the recital continues in an unbroken melody and at the conclusion, a few verses are recited in adoration of Bhagavan himself.

The prayers over, there is an hour to get ready for the morning coffee. The low lying Arunachala Hill looks singularly beautiful in the light of the dawn and one is aware of that harmony between man and nature which is so essential to balanced life. As one strolls out of the Ashram one is aware that Tiruvannamalai is a town of sacred memories, of temples small and big, and of graveyards dedicated to the memories of the departed. There are shrines, some modest and some more pretentious, built all around the Hill, but the greatest monument of them all  is the superb temple of Arunachalam.

It was interesting to learn that the custom of burial was and still is not uncommon among certain classes of people in the south. Unfortunately however, the memorial stones are scattered on the periphery of the town and are in a state of complete neglect, as is also the case with some beautiful *mandapams* and temples of all sizes. It could not have been the decline of the devout spirit so much as the weakening and disintegration of economic life which, once so prosperous as to have built the great edifices, is now no longer able even to afford their maintenance. The people are poor because perhaps they have not been able to keep pace with the march of time. In the whole of Tiruvannamalai the living centre is the modest Ashram of Bhagavan, for here the spiritual lamp stays burning, capable of igniting the fires in the hearts of those who are still wanting or are prepared to receive the illumination.

It was fortunate that the next day of our halt at the Ashram was the sacred day of *Maha Shivaratri*. Very early in the morning crowds of people were on the march around the sacred Hill of Arunachalam and in the Ashram itself worship was continuous for all the twenty four hours. The great temple of Arunachalam was illuminated but the resources of the people were far too attenuated to permit adequate lighting. One day when the people of India are again strong and economically prosperous these temples will perhaps, be revived into centres of inspiration and light, and their vast *mandapams* might be restored to their proper use and status.

We attended the evening prayers on the eve of our departure. There could be no farewell, for Bhagavan's presence would never be forgotten. We bade mental farewell to the Ashram for we were going to leave for Pondicherry early next morning. As we were about to leave, a friend said that we could not possibly leave the Ashram without taking the permission of Bhagavan and saying goodbye to him. We therefore repaired to the Ashram to intimate our departure to Bhagavan just as he was going out of the dining hall. We felt like young children going to their elders for a blessing. Our reward, however, was immense, for Bhagavan vouchsafed to us a penetrating glance of immeasurable beatitude which, even now, is one of the most abiding memories of a sacred pilgrimage. It is astonishing how Bhagavan's presence and his usual, apparently humdrum activities cast such a magic spell over all those who were blessed to come near him.

# BHAGAVAN RAMANA MAHARSHI AS SEEN BY A BENGALI DEVOTEE

## Jagannath Chattopadhyaya

TO A BENGALI who has been accustomed to hear the Lord's name chanted with fervour and devotion, accompanied by dancing and *sankirtan,* as introduced into Bengal by Lord Gouranga more than four hundred years ago, Bhagavan's method of enquiry in absolute stillness of the mind, presents a sharp contrast. In the life of Bhagavan I am confronted with a towering personality, the like of which I have never seen or heard of or come across in books.

He never ran down any religion or the traditions sponsored by a religion. For instance, the Hindu caste system has become the target of criticism by preachers and reformers but Bhagavan would never attack it outright. When asked whether we should ignore caste rules he said, "Not in the beginning. Observe them to start with. They serve as a check on the vagaries of the mind and it is thus purified. On the same subject he says, "Differences always exist, not only in human beings but also in plants, animals, etc. This state of affairs cannot be helped. You need not notice these distinctions. There is diversity in the world but a unity runs through the diversity. The Self is the same in all. There is no difference in spirit. The differences are external and superficial. Find the unity and you will be happy."1

I myself am a disciple of Sri Sitaramdas Omkarnath Maharaj, the strict follower of *sanatana dharma*, the eternal *dharma* based on the *Vedas* and *Upanishads*, to which foreigners have given the name 'Hinduism'. He is also an upholder of our *varnashrama dharma* or caste *dharma*. I therefore very much appreciate the Maharshi's respect for every religion. Once, for instance, he told a Muslim devotee to try to understand and follow what the word 'Islam' means — 'the total surrender of the ego'.

Bhagavan's courageous message, reminding us of our heritage of the *rishis* of old, gives us faith and courage despite the gloom of present day materialism, to seek liberation from bondage to the non-self, the fake ego, which causes the sorrows and frustrations of life.

ॐ ૐ

# REMEMBERING RAMANA

## N. N. Rajan

## I

## Miracles and Bhagavan

IT IS COMMON to see people flock to those who exhibit occult powers and perform miracles like curing ailments, floating on water, sitting buried under earth etc. but Self-realisation and miracle mongering are poles apart. The *jnani* does not care for miracles. To the *jnani* the control of the senses leading to realisation of the Self is the only aim. This is really the greatest miracle, and to achieve it is the *jnani's* goal.

The great *jnani* that he was, Bhagavan Sri Ramana always revelled in the natural state of supreme bliss. He did not wish to perform miracles. In fact, he warned people against it. This does not mean that he had no powers. He had them in abundance, as witnessed by many, only Bhagavan never liked to exhibit them.

He behaved as any ordinary man would. Regarding the manifestation of powers seen by devotees, it might be due to his infinite compassion that the miracles happened and he might not have been particularly intent on them.

One evening, while I was sitting outside Sri Bhagavan's hall, just in his view, suddenly I noticed an expressive gesture in his face as he leaned forward from his reclining position. It looked as though he was calling me to say something. I was impelled to respond to the gesture by getting up and going near him but he did not tell me anything. I resumed my seat only to find, in a couple of minutes, another jerk and a similar expressive movement in him as before. This time also I was stirred and when I went nearer there was no further indication. I took my seat again but now became restless. I could not resist the urge to leave the place at once with the expectation of some urgent matter demanding my presence. I prostrated to Sri Bhagavan and I left the hall without a word.

A major train accident had happened at my headquarters station about nine miles off. I had been forewarned by Bhagavan in a strange manner as recorded above and due to his grace, I was free from the blame of not being on the spot in the emergency. Obviously Bhagavan's warning was quite in advance of the actual happening. The way he did it is most noteworthy. There was no public demonstration or publicity. An act of grace to a devotee, in his own unique way and with no means of others knowing that a miracle was actually performed. This is typical of our Bhagavan.

# II

# His Divine Excellence

"SRI RAMANA MAHARSHI has kept India's spiritual glory alive in our generation. He has in his own way made the name of India respected by wise and enlightened men spread all over the world......"

Thus spoke Sri C. Rajagopalachari when declaring open the Pathala Lingam Shrine, once the abode of Sri Ramana Maharshi.

Bhagavan Sri Ramana Maharshi encapsulated the whole of the Vedas and Upanishads into a simple formula — his famous 'Who am I?' enquiry. He was too humble to claim any originality for this. Such enquiry goes beyond the realm of seemingly impenetrable mysteries. But by the grace of Sri Ramana his followers unmistakably reach the goal.

During the period of his illness Sri Maharshi appeared visibly unaffected in spite of the ailment which gave him excruciating pain. The doctors and other devotees were baffled by the utmost unconcern demonstrated by Sri Maharshi for the cruel ailment. The total detachment with which he looked on his suffering body was unique. By this he demonstrated practically for our benefit that only the body suffers and the *Atman* (Self) has no share in it.

His radiant face did not show even the least trace of pain. In fact his eyes sparkled with more divine brilliance than usual. Despite the pain he was rigidly attending to his daily routine, like going to the bathroom, attending to important letters, etc., without deviating from his characteristic punctuality. "Let the disease run its course and let the body suffer, but I am ever immersed in unbroken Bliss" — such was his attitude.

"A man established in the Self is liberated while in the body, the fate of the body does not matter": this is the Vedic truth. Sri Ramana had entirely forgotten all consciousness about his occupancy in the human frame and automatically the authorship had no existence at all. He was full of bliss indicating exuberance. The following episode, which occurred during the same period was a thrilling sight to witness.

An old teacher of Sri Bhagavan came to see him. He was 87 and very feeble. Nevertheless an overmastering desire to see the God-man whom he had once taught in second form, urged him on to Tiruvannamalai. In Bhagavan's presence, he recalled an incident from that time with great emotion. Once he had asked young Venkataraman to stand up on the bench for a minor misdemeanour. But Venkataraman gazed at him for a while with such steadiness and power that his (teacher's) will withered rapidly and he reversed his decision.

It was a touching sight to see the old teacher meet his Seer-pupil. Then the teacher asked Sri Bhagavan whether he recognised him. Sri Bhagavan smiled broadly and graciously and answered: "Why not?" The teacher was visibly moved at this and he again asked Bhagavan about his health. Sri Bhagavan replied that he was feeling all right. Throughout this very moving but short interview Maharshi displayed such graciousness and cordiality that neither the old teacher nor those who were close by felt that there was anything wrong with the Maharshi.

These things make us feel that Bhagavan Sri Ramana Maharshi is a perfect divine incarnation, whose divine excellence was lying dormant till he left his home.

ॐ ॐ

# THE FORTUNATE BOY

## "SEIN"

BHAGAVAN SRI RAMANA MAHARSHI is well known to all as a great Saint. But only a few know of his philanthropy and humanitarianism. Still fewer are those who experienced his paternal and maternal affection.

Of all these one boy alone had the most enviable opportunity of sleeping with Bhagavan and enjoying such paternal treatment. One and only one had that golden privilege.

This was in 1920. Bhagavan had come to Skandasramam from the Virupaksha cave and a small batch of devotees had gathered round him. The greatness of the Saint echoed all over the world. Devotees from all parts of India were coming for his *darshan*. While males enjoyed the privilege of staying in the Asramam up the hill with Bhagavan the whole day, ladies were not allowed to remain there after sun-set.

Maharshi had a younger brother and sister, his elder brother having passed away prematurely. This younger brother Sri Nagasundaram Iyer who was working as a clerk in Tiruvengadu temple had a small son. Fortunately for Sri Ramanasramam to be and unfortunately for his family, he took *sannyasa* when his wife died leaving a two year old boy uncared for. When both the parents left this child an orphan, Maharshi's sister, popularly known as 'Athai' (aunt), took charge of the child and brought him up with unstinted love, affection and care. It was not only because she had no issue of her own but also because this boy was the only descendant of their whole family.

This lad was taken twice or thrice a year to Tiruvannamalai to see Bhagavan and his father (of the *poorvasrama*), henceforth known as Sri Niranjanananda Swami, by Athai and her husband, who were living in the far South. They were provided with a house near the hill at Tiruvannamalai. Every morning Athai would go up the hill and return to town in the evening, leaving the boy behind at Skandasramam.

When at first Athai hesitated to do this fearing to cause any kind of inconvenience to the much loved boy, Bhagavan said that he would be well under his protection.

In the night the boy would eat from the sacred hands of Bhagavan and Bhagavan would make him lie down beside him, cover him with a blanket and lull him to sleep. He bestowed on him all care that any sincere mother is capable of. Early in the morning he would take the boy to the spring, clean his teeth with powder, and wash his face. Athai would rush up in the morning. Bhagavan with the lad seated on a culvert would tell the child, "There comes your Athai. See in what hurry she runs up to see you." As soon as she came up, Bhagavan would tell her, "Take your boy, see, he is safe and sound."

This abundant affection for the boy did not in any way prevent Maharshi from being strict with him. The following incident makes it clear that Bhagavan gave the boy a practical lesson which till now he has not forgotten.

At Skandasramam lived a monkey named Nondi, which was the pet of all. Maharshi had ordered that whatever food was served to his followers should also be served to the monkey, and in case it was absent elsewhere, then its share should be kept separate for its return. In such a case, the food would be kept near a window inside the cave and the shutter closed but not bolted. This was the custom.

◆ On one of his periodical visits to the Asramam one day, the boy had enjoyed the sweet dishes served to the devotees. He had a little more than the usual share. The monkey being absent, its share was kept near the closed window. The boy, having had his share, went up to the window and began to eat out of the monkey's as well. Suddenly, the monkey came and opened the window only to see the boy eating its share. It gave the boy a blow on his cheek. Shocked and terrified, the boy cried out and devotees tried to console him. Bhagavan came to the spot, understood the situation and told the boy: "You deserve it. Why did you want his (monkey's) share. You have had enough already. You ought to have been contented with that." Instead of appeasing the beloved child, Bhagavan put him right. The boy became silent and heeded Bhagavan's words.

"Do not touch the property of others. Be content with what you have. Share equally what you have. Divide it with one and all around you. Help the needy. Be not blind when a wrong is committed before you. Correct it if possible, or at least speak out for the right." These are some of the golden truths the young boy was able to grasp from the words of the Maharshi that day.

That blessed boy is Swami Ramanananda (Sri T.N. Venkataraman, former president of Sri Ramanasramam, the only descendant of Maharshi's family).

౪ ౩

# LEST WE FORGET ...

## I

## Dr. V. Srinivasa Rao

AMONG THE FOREMOST DEVOTEES, Dr. V. Srinivasa Rao found in Sri Bhagavan the greatest solace and support in his life. He was born in the former native state of Pudukottai and is happily still with us at the age of eighty-seven(in1972). He was intimately associated with the growth of the Ashram for many decades. Childlike by nature and outspoken, his sincerity and frankness gained him easy access and familiarity with Sri Bhagavan who treated him like a pet child.

Born poor and orphaned when hardly four years old, he grew up to be self-reliant. He took his degree in medicine and surgery, and prompted by the good wishes of the doyen of his days, Dr. Singaravelu Mudaliar, he entered Government service. He was medical officer in several district headquarters hospitals and retired in 1940 as the superintendent of the Royapettah Hospital, Madras. After this he spent a good deal of his time in the Ashram in a life of devotion and service to Sri Bhagavan.

To begin with, Dr. Srinivasa Rao had no interest in a spiritual life and seemed more an agnostic, if not a downright atheist. Through the friendship of spiritually highly evolved people like Sri S. Doraiswami Iyer, one of the oldest devotees, he came to Sri

Bhagavan. Before taking leave of Sri Bhagavan he asked him, "Will I come again for your *darshan*?" Sri Bhagavan with a tender and compassionate look patted him on the shoulder saying, "What will happen is sure to happen." That was all! He felt somehow thrilled in the core of his being by his touch and the gracious reply which strengthened his faith and surrender. Since then remembrance of Sri Bhagavan was constant.

Sri Bhagavan directed his attention specifically to *Upadesa Saram* among his works and emphasised *ekachintana* (fixing the mind on one thought — of the One) as essential for the mind to get free of thoughts; and that constant remembrance of God is better than a recital of hymns or silent invocation. On one occasion he told Sri Bhagavan, "It is said that one should contemplate on God Vishnu from head to foot. Is that the correct thing to do?" Sri Bhagavan reminded him, "It is all One from head to foot." Yet again he discussed the efficacy of *Rama Japa* and the like and asked Sri Bhagavan, "Why not do *Ramana Japa* instead of *Rama Japa?*" to which Sri Bhagavan gave his assent.

After 1940 Srinivasa Rao had the unique opportunity of staying in the proximity of Sri Bhagavan rendering some personal service or other. He treasures the privilege he had of massaging Sri Bhagavan's limbs and of ministering to him during his bodily ailments as a doctor. His simple but total love and attachment to Sri Bhagavan's person generated many happy incidents. Once Sri Bhagavan's knee caps and legs did not function owing to stiffness and Srinivasa Rao with folded hands implored him to permit his massaging for a few days only. Sri Bhagavan would not agree saying, "If allowed to do so you will continue endlessly." But he beseeched him like a child and Sri Bhagavan yielded but said it would be strictly for ten days. Sri Bhagavan was counting the days and on the last day when Srinivasa Rao was actually massaging his legs Sri T. P. R.'s father who arrived just then, entered the old hall and perceiving the doctor massaging the legs of Sri Bhagavan repeated a Sanskrit *sloka* and exclaimed, "Oh, Raoji, do not give up what you are doing. You need no other *sadhana* for your salvation." Sri Bhagavan burst out laughing and said: "Well, well; I have been counting these days and waiting for this last day and you have come to recommend continuance!" Leaving his massaging, the doctor stepped before Sri Bhagavan and went on doing obeisance imploring Him to listen to the elderly gentleman if not to him. Sri Bhagavan yielded for another ten days!

During the two years preceding Sri Bhagavan's *Maha Nirvana* the doctor gave whole-time attention and assistance to Sri Bhagavan's health and comfort in collaboration with the team of medical men who devoutly rendered service during the last illness.

He happily spent his days remembering Sri Bhagavan and his memorable days with him, and deriving all the solace needed from his writings and utterances, which he revered.

# II

## G. Lakshmi Narasimham

SRI G. LAKSHMI NARASIMHAM (known as ' Narasinga Rao' at the Ashram), after taking his B.L. degree stayed at Sri Ramanasramam for three years from 1930 to 1933, along with his mother and sister Lakshmi, serving Sri Bhagavan. It was Bhagavan's Grace that his apprenticeship should be under him.

Lakshmi Narasimham's marriage also took place at Tiruvannamalai and when the new couple came to do *namaskaram* (prostration), Sri Bhagavan remarked: "Now, your name (Lakshmi + Narasimham) has become meaningful!"

Sri Niranjanananda Swami (also known as Chinnaswami, Sri Bhagavan's brother) was the Manager of the Ashram then and his office was near Bhagavan's Hall. Like others Narasinga Rao also was meditating in Bhagavan's Hall. Chinnaswami asked him to assist him in the Ashram correspondence. Getting Bhagavan's approval for it, Narasinga Rao began going straight to Chinnaswami after bowing to Bhagavan. Later on this earned the humorous remark of Bhagavan: "Oh! He belongs to Chinnaswami, not to the Hall group!"

Chinnaswami was a strict and conscientious taskmaster. He spared no pains in keeping an exact account of money received and spent. He looked upon Bhagavan not as his brother but as God Himself, and so considered it his first duty to serve Bhagavan's devotees, accommodating them and attending to their wants. The temple, the big dining hall and well furnished accommodations are the results of his labour of love. Actually seeing Chinnaswami's one pointed spirit of service, G.L.N. dedicated himself to serve him to the best of his ability, surrendering himself thus to Bhagavan. Saraswati Ammal and Lakshmi used to do their bit of service in the kitchen. From their experience too they were led to conclude that whatever Chinnaswami did had always the distinct approval of Bhagavan.

Gradually all the members of Narasinga Rao's family became attached to Sri Bhagavan and the Ashram, by bonds of devotion and reverence. They all regarded Chinnaswami as a true instrument of Bhagavan. His eldest brother, the late Sambasiva Rao, was a reputed lawyer of Nellore. Till he passed away in 1962, he diligently served the Ashram in the legal and other spheres. Sister Lakshmi and brother-in-law, B. S. Ranganadham, are great devotees of Bhagavan. His third elder brother, the late Satyanarayana Rao, a teacher at the Mahant's High School, Vellore, from about 1925, was the first to be drawn to Bhagavan and it was his influence which brought other members of the family to Bhagavan. He was deeply devoted to Bhagavan and was blessed with the proximity and touch of grace of Bhagavan during his last illness within the Ashram premises. His fourth brother, the late Subba Rao, a teacher at Nellore, used to assist with his Scout troup during Bhagavan's *Jayanti* celebrations. These celebrations and the taking out of Bhagavan's picture in procession, started by him, continue up to this day at Nellore.

When G. L. N. came to the Ashram, he did not know even a letter of the Tamil alphabet. Impelled by Bhagavan's grace he picked up enough knowledge of Tamil to read and understand Sri Bhagavan's works in the original. Thus it was nothing but Bhagavan's grace that enabled him- to translate into Telugu Bhagavan's *Five Hymns to Arunachala* and *Forty Verses on Reality*.

Chinnaswami intuitively hit upon some devotees to help him and trusted them completely. For instance, when he went to Rangoon in 1936 to personally select and purchase special teak wood for the construction of Sri Matrubhuteswara Temple, he put Narasinga Rao in charge of the Ashram during his absence of over a month. During the life-time of Bhagavan and Chinnaswami and even after, right up to the end, Narasinga Rao had been a devoted servant of the Ashram.

ॐ ఊ

# HOW I CAME TO BHAGAVAN

## I

## Roda MacIver

I HEARD ABOUT Sri Bhagavan for the first time in 1939 from a friend who showed me his photograph. I was very much struck by his eyes and wished to go and see him. My desire to go to Tiruvannamalai to Sri Bhagavan's abode could not be fulfilled until 1942. A friend, who had just finished building a house in Tiruvannamalai invited me to stay with her. I eagerly accepted the invitation. When I arrived I was indisposed for a few days and could not go to the Ashram. I heard that Sri Bhagavan was in the habit of going for a walk on the hill of Arunachala every day at regular hours, so I went there and waited on the path. On the crest of the hilly path a head emerged like the rising sun and then I saw the whole majestic tall figure, Bhagavan Sri Ramana Maharshi! Slowly he came towards me, his attendant a few steps behind. He stopped for a few moments before me, smiling and looking at me graciously. My heart was beating fast and I could not utter a word. I cannot describe how I felt really. I experienced a coolness.

During the next two years I was visiting the Ashram constantly. Then in 1944 one day I went into the hall. Sri Bhagavan was reading some papers. I sat down and looked at him. Suddenly he put away the papers and turned his luminous eyes on me. I could not stand his gaze so I closed my eyes, tears streaming down my face. When I opened my eyes he was still looking at me. My heart was flooded with joy and an inner calmness! Later I went to see a friend of mine, Sri Munagala Venkataramiah,[1] and told him in detail about this occurrence in the hall. He said that I was very fortunate to have received initiation from Sri Bhagavan. There was no doubt about it!

Next morning when I was in the hall somebody asked Sri Bhagavan what was the use of sitting before him. Does he give initiation? Sri Bhagavan replied that initiation can be given in three ways: by silence, by look and by touch. When saying "by look", he looked at me. Then I remembered what I was told the day before about my experience and had no doubt that I had received initiation from Sri Bhagavan, my most revered Master!

After a month's stay I returned to Bombay, and there was a complete change in my life. Worldly pleasures ceased to attract me and I wanted to be alone as much as possible. I decided to leave Bombay and settle down in Tiruvannamalai but did not know where to stay. It was difficult in those days to get accommodation but I knew Sri Bhagavan was guiding me and so I did not worry much. He would arrange everything. And it so happened that two days before leaving Bombay I met my husband to be. He told me to go and stay in his house in Tiruvannamalai and so I left happily. Soon after, with Sri Bhagavan's blessings, we got married and this house became my permanent home.

---

[1] Later known as Swami Ramanananda Saraswati, compiler of *Talks with Sri Ramana Maharshi* and author of other books.

By Bhagavan's grace I am now permanently settled here and do not intend to leave. He still helps and guides me as before and often hears my prayers. His Presence now is even more powerful than when he was in the physical body.

My love for Sri Bhagavan sustains me and is of the greatest importance in my life!

# II

## M. S. Nagarajan

SRI M.S. NAGARAJAN, a staunch devotee of Bhagavan, comes from Mambattu, a village in the Polur Taluk of the North Arcot District of the state of Tamil Nadu. Even as a young boy he used to accompany his parents when they came to Tiruvannamalai for the yearly Deepam festival, at which time and on similar occasions, his father, who was a devotee of Bhagavan, used to take him to the Ashram. Thus he came to know Bhagavan in his childhood. When he was ten years old, his friend, who was a nephew of Echammal, spoke to him about the greatness of Bhagavan. He and this friend used to practise *dhyana* and yogic *asanas* (sitting postures) every day in the early morning. In the evening they meditated on Bhagavan. Sri Nagarajan used to have frequent visions of Bhagavan and Lord Murugan in his dreams. At about this time Ranga Rao, an old devotee of Bhagavan, now no more, had set up an ashram at Polur named Indra Ashram, to which other devotees of Bhagavan used to go and talk about Bhagavan and other spiritual matters. In 1930, when Sri Nagarajan was 15 years old Ranga Rao brought him to Sri Ramanansramam. Here he was allotted the work of doing *puja*, and helping in the bookstall etc. But what he valued most was the privilege of cutting up vegetables and grinding the pulses and coconut gratings for chutney in the kitchen with Bhagavan. But most of the time he was in the hall attending to some minor work or other. He had thus the opportunity of listening to the replies which Bhagavan gave to the questions put to him by visitors and devotees. As a result of this he became a firm believer in the path of Self-enquiry taught by Bhagavan.

At the end of six months Sri Nagarajan went home but soon returned and stayed on for four years. Jobs were offered to him but he was not interested in them since the acceptance of a job would mean parting from Bhagavan. But one day a letter came from his mother informing him that a job had been found for him. This letter came to the hands of Bhagavan along with the Ashram post. After reading it Bhagavan said, "Look here, a job has been found for you. Go and accept it immediately." Tears came into the eyes of Sri Nagarajan at the thought of parting from Bhagavan. But Bhagavan said again, "You can go on Wednesday and join duty on Thursday." Unwillingly he left the Ashram. Thereafter he came to the Ashram as often as he could get leave.

While Sri Nagarajan was employed at Sattur from 1955 to 1958 he organised a Ramana *Mandali* where Bhagavan's songs like *The Marital Garland of Letters* were sung and devotees meditated every day. Talks were given periodically at this *Mandali* — Bhagavan's *Jayanti* and *Aradhana* were also celebrated in a fitting manner. Sri Nagarajan also established a school named Sri Ramana Vidya Mandiram Elementary School at Sattur in memory of Bhagavan.

After holding several important posts in the firm of Burmah Shell, Sri Nagarajan has now retired. Since then he has lived for some time in Tambaram and later joined the Ashram to render his service.

# III

# A Seeker

THIS IS OFFERED as homage to Sri Ramana and as testimony to the truth that all paths lead to the same Peak and that without Grace there is nothing, neither "light" nor "darkness", neither "regress" nor "progress"; Grace is All.

Born into a non-religious Jewish family, I was raised in a small Protestant town in the southern United States. At twenty I found myself in a university in the Northeast and extremely unhappy. Till then God had meant nothing to me; but abruptly things changed. Some Higher Intelligence began hammering me over the head with the fact of Its existence and by moving me through coincidences in which the whole universe seemed to converge in direct answers to my innermost questions of the moment.

That summer I read an autobiography of a yogi. It electrified me, literally: after reading it I lay relaxed before sleep, wondering if yoga were to be part of my path. An oscillating sound came to me and raised my mind inwardly; suddenly there sounded an incredibly beautiful herald of trumpets followed by a flash of brilliant light which illuminated my whole being.

Needless to say, I took this as a "yes" to my question, and that fall I took initiation from a disciple of an enlightened Indian yogi. By the next summer I felt ready to go to India. I wasn't able to leave till autumn.

This Master, called Baba, lived up to all my expectations, and more. He showered his grace upon me; my prayers for greater devotion were being answered. But then something happened which I cannot detail. Here through his words, actions, and arrangement of my "external" circumstances, he indicated unmistakably that I was to leave his mission, perhaps never to see him again physically. So I left.

Before departing from India a friend and I visited other ashrams. The message I got was: all paths are one; and the Guru is within, so seek within. I went halfway across the world to find someone to save me, but those capable merely referred me to a mirror.

Thus I returned to the States, feeling exalted by a wondrous journey — it was a perfect circle of experience — but also somewhat confused as to how to proceed. I was reading Krishnamurti and trying to Be, but I didn't feel comfortable or secure in a practice which said, "Make no effort." I was praying to Jesus. Shortly after my return, I had met a devotee of Jesus who asked if I had accepted Him in my heart. I quickly answered, "Yes"; but upon reflection I realized that was untrue. So I was praying very fervently to Jesus, that He enter my heart.

At the same time I was praying to my first Guru ("my" Guru's first form). I had come to feel that I could be satisfied with nothing less than absolute and eternal Realization. It felt almost blasphemous to ask so much, but what else could I ask?

So all this was going on, and at the height of it Baba came to me in a dream. I was sitting before him in *darshan* with a few others. He asked if I had been practising a certain *mantra*. Anxious to please him, I blurted "Yes". He said sternly, "No, you haven't," and looked away. I began to weep, my head against his knee. Then something made me look up at him. Smiling, he said simply, "Yours is the path of the Heart."

Upon awakening I thought he might have been referring to the occasional feelings in the centre of my chest that were accompanying my practice of trying to BE with all things. Or maybe he meant something in reference to my prayer to Jesus. I didn't know, and nothing was made clear.

By late spring I was feeling pretty miserable. No changes, no breakthroughs. Some friends and I had attempted to establish a community; egoism aborted it. I was often on the verge of tears. One weekend I visited some friends on a farm, people I had met in India. But rather than feeling any *satsang*, I felt a loneliness, even paranoia, that I thought I'd left behind long ago. After two days of this misery, I picked up a little pamphlet, "Who am I?", with a picture of the slender young Ramana. By reading it I was able at least to regain my equilibrium.

The next night, at a friend's apartment in Montreal, Quebec, I came across *The Teachings of Bhagavan* by Arthur Osborne. By now quite interested, I read parts of it and then tried the *sadhana* the Maharshi recommended. After fifteen or twenty minutes of asking mentally, "Who am I?", and concentrating on the right side of my chest, suddenly, from the depths of my Heart something opened up in me, a piercing sensation followed by a wave of bliss. The bliss passed, and the piercing sensation diminished over the next few days — but the feeling of the Heart remained.

Since then It has never left me — though sometimes I leave It for this thought or that, and It remains on the edge of consciousness. Shortly after Its advent I came to see that this is the path of the Heart, and that I shall have to find no other forms for my Guru. And then it dawned on me that my prayer to Jesus had been answered. For as it is true that no one other than Sri Ramana vibrates at the Core of my Being, so also it is no one other than Jesus, and no one other than Baba.

"Ask, and ye shall receive; seek, and ye shall find." "Earnest efforts never fail." What else is there to say? Full realization has not dawned, but whether moments or lifetimes intervene, it cannot fail to come. Patience and perseverance are necessary, as Bhagavan has said. It may take long years of practice to reach the Goal.

Yet the Grace he has bestowed upon me compels me to conclude on a different note. For Bhagavan again says we are the Self, ever and always; and Jesus says be alert, for you don't know when the Bridegroom will arrive. And indeed, young Venkataraman experienced the truth of this latter statement most dramatically, at the moment of his death and the arrival of the Bridegroom, Arunachala. So we should be patient and persevering, but we shouldn't give a moment's thought to "the long years ahead" and other such poison. For "the thought that you are not realized is the obstacle to Realization." If we don't feel we know Reality, ever and always, then we must at least feel continuously that its lightning flash is imminent. Such an attitude naturally allows *sadhana* to become the all-consuming flame it should be, and thus "hastens" the Coming. For, again as Venkataraman realized, no one walks that final infinite distance to the Peak of Arunachala — but rather, in a way too inscrutable for the mind to comprehend, and at a speed far too fast for the ego to withstand, one is brought to the Heart-Summit by the Mountain Itself.

# BHAGAVAN'S SOLICITUDE FOR DEVOTEES

## Kunju Swami

*An old and well-known devotee of Bhagavan describes some instances of Bhagavan's solicitude for his devotees, especially for women and old people.*

BHAGAVAN WAS ALWAYS very considerate towards his devotees in all matters. When he was living at Skandashram on the eastern slopes of the hill, he used to wake up at 3 o'clock in the morning. He would not get up immediately but recline on the bed. We too would wake up at the same time and sit in meditation near him. Bhagavan's mother used to sing some devotional songs from within. Bhagavan's routine was to go out at half past four and return by five. We would then begin to recite the *Aksharamana Malai* (The Marital Garland of Letters). That was the only song which Bhagavan had composed at that time. I learned it by heart by merely listening to the chanting of the other devotees. The recitation was over by six o'clock which was the time for Bhagavan to go for his bath.

There was a large flat stone at the spot where now there is the low wall on the eastern side. Tooth powder and water were kept on it for Bhagavan's use. In all weathers he used to sit on it facing the east and clean his teeth. His body was glowing in the rays of the rising sun. If there was heavy dew we tried to dissuade him from sitting there, but without any success. Nor did he tell us the reason for sitting there always. It was some time afterwards that we came to know of it.

An old woman named Saubhagyathammal, living in a house near the foot of the hill, and some of her friends had made it a daily practice not to take any food until they had had *darshan* of Bhagavan and Sri Seshadri Swami. They used to come up to Skandashram every day for this purpose. One day Saubhagyathammal did not come. If any of his regular devotees were absent on any particular day Bhagavan never failed to make enquiries and find out the reason. So when the old woman came the next day he asked her why she did not come on the previous day. She replied,"I had Sri Bhagavan's *darshan* yesterday." "But you did not come yesterday", said Bhagavan. "Bhagavan knew that this humble devotee was too feeble to climb the hill and so he made it possible for her to see him from a place close to her house", was the reply. She explained that she had seen Bhagavan while he was sitting on the stone and cleaning his teeth and said that she was henceforth going to have his *darshan* everyday in the same way. From that time onwards Bhagavan made it a practice to sit on that stone for nearly half an hour daily. Later on when Bhagavan took up his abode at the foot of the hill it was also chiefly out of consideration for his aged devotees who found it difficult to climb to Skandashram. After the passing away of his mother he occasionally came down to her *samadhi*. Aged devotees eagerly awaited these opportunities to see him. And so when they begged him to remain below he began to live there permanently.

It was the practice of Bhagavan's devotees to take his permission before proceeding to circumambulate the hill and to prostrate before him on their return. Many came to the Ashram all the way from the town for this purpose even late in the evening and then proceeded immediately to their homes in the town. Bhagavan advised such devotees to break their circumambulation in town in the evening and to complete it on the following day when they came to the Ashram as usual.

When women devotees were ready to return to town at dusk he would always make certain that none of them went alone. If any of them found no company he would ask someone to go with her and leave her at her house.

There were some devotees employed in Madras who used to come every weekend to Tiruvannamalai and return to Madras in time to go to their offices on Monday morning. Sometimes some of them were so reluctant to part from Bhagavan that they continued to overstay their time. They would go as far as the railway station only to return to the Ashram on some pretext or other. Bhagavan, therefore, used in such cases to send someone with them to the railway station and see that they actually got into the train and left for Madras. He did not like that anyone should neglect his duties!

When a devotee came late in the evening after every one had taken his meal and gone to bed he was not allowed to go hungry on this account. Bhagavan always saw to it that some food was kept for such late-comers and that they had their meal. When such a visitor arrived Bhagavan simply looked at some of us. That was enough for us to take him to the dining hall and give him his meal!

Bhagavan never started to eat before all those who were present were served. The beggars waiting at the gate are even now given their food before inmates and visitors are served. No exception is made to this rule even on crowded occasions like the *Jayanthi* and the *Aradhana*. All these instances will show how considerate Bhagavan was to others!

# Reminiscences

## I

## A. Venkateswara Sarma and Smt. Sala

SRI VENKATESWARA SARMA, a native of Keelapasalai Village, Ramnad Dt., is an old devotee of Sri Bhagavan, who along with his wife, Smt. Sala, equally devoted to Sri Bhagavan, lived in Sri Ramana Nagar. Both are closely related to Sri Bhagavan.

For over a decade he studied the Kavya (poetical literature in Sanskrit) gaining mastery in the same and also became an adept in the science of astrology by training he had for years at Vidyalaya in Kerala. In his early days while staying at Kandanur, he had a remarkable experience. He saw the portrait of Sri Bhagavan in his majestic standing posture with a penetrating look which not merely seemed but was really felt as directed only to him and which thrilled his whole being. This experience provoked a great urge to have Sri Bhagavan's *darshan* immediately.

He started the very next day and arrived at Tiruvannamalai, his luggage consisting of a *panchangam* (almanac) in one hand and an umbrella in the other. That was in 1920. He climbed up the hill to Skandashram, and recognising Sri Bhagavan who was seated then under a nelli tree he hastened to prostrate at his feet, spontaneously reciting in a state of ecstatic inspiration the first *sloka* of *Sri Dakshinamurthi Ashtakam*. "Look, look at the visitor who has come — Subbu's son, is it not?" So exclaimed Sri Bhagavan, turning to his mother who was there. The mother gave him a hearty welcome and made him feel at home. Delighted by the stay with Sri Bhagavan that night, he was guided to perform *giripradakshina* (circumambulation of Holy Arunachala) next day. He expressed an ardent desire to stay with Sri Bhagavan for good and pleaded that he did not want to marry but wished to remain with him and serve him and do *pujas*. The mother would have none of it, he had duties to perform, she reminded him and an uncle's daughter awaited marriage with him. He was then 22 years old. Sri Bhagavan consoled him, "What does it matter if you do *puja* or get married or whether you are here or elsewhere?" And so he left!

Since then Sri Sarma was coming to Sri Bhagavan from time to time, often staying for a month or two and benefitting by Sri Bhagavan's utterances and his silent influence with devotion and piety.

Though a successful astrologer by profession, especially in the branch of *prasna* (astrological forecasting on the basis of the exact time of the client's question), Sri Venkateswara Sarma felt the futility of leading a bread-earning life and hence came to Sri Ramanasramam in 1939, along with his wife, and lived with Sri Bhagavan's sister's family. In 1946 they took up abode at Adi Annamalai, four miles away from the Ashram on the circumambulation path, after duly informing Sri Bhagavan. They went round the hill daily and sometimes twice a day and thus had *darshan* of Sri Bhagavan on the way.

Sri Sarma compiled a short history of Sri Bhagavan's life consisting of 120 slokas in Sanskrit, known as *Ramana Charitamrutasaram*, which Sri Bhagavan graciously perused and corrected. He also composed songs in Tamil and presented them to Sri Bhagavan, who used to correct them only sparingly. Such corrections were not only grammatical in content but also vitally enriched them with spiritual depth. For instance, in the following verse: "Those who are caught in the mouth of a great tiger are certain to die in this world; but all those, caught in the glance (*drishti*) of the great tiger adorning the slopes of Arunachala, known as great Ramana, get merged with natural ease in the eternal happiness, discarding fear of even the Lord of Death," Sri Bhagavan put in the word with natural ease '(*iyal*) in the place of daily' (*nidham*) of Sri Sarma's!

Since 1948, he settled with his wife and only son in Tiruvannamalai town. The son passed away four years later. Both parents feel they survived that shock only by Bhagavan's Grace. They continued to render service at the Shrines of Sri Bhagavan and the Mother, assisting in the daily routine — perhaps as a fulfilment of his former *sankalpa* (desire) to do *puja* to Sri Bhagavan! He felt: "Sri Bhagavan is ever present in my mind and heart, in *jagrat* and *swapna* and his manifest Grace only is sustaining us in all circumstances and at all times!"

# II

## M. S. Nagarajan

SRI BHAGAVAN HAD a unique method of expounding profound truths with illustrations taken from everyday life. His words were never premeditated but came spontaneously, they were also apt, as the following incident will show.

It was in 1932, I think, when I was in charge of the daily *puja* at the Mother's shrine, that a devotee known as P.W.D. Ramaswami Iyer arranged for a special food offering of *sarkarai pongal* (a kind of rice-pudding) and *vadai* (a small round cake of blackgram fried in oil). They were to be offered at the time of the *ushah puja* (puja conducted before day break in the month of Margasira (December-January)). I had many things to do and there was no one to help me. So I got up very early, at about half past three, and after taking my bath in the Pali Tirtham, removed the old flowers from the shrine, swept and cleaned the floor and lit two fires, over one of which I placed the pot of rice for the *pongal* and over the other the pan of oil for the *vadai*. I then sat down to grind the black gram which I had soaked in water previously. By the time the dough was ready, the oil was sufficiently hot. I had not actually prepared *vadais* previously at any time. But I took some dough and tried to spread it out on the leaf in the form of a neat round *vadai* as I had seen others do, but it would not come out properly. I tried again and again but it was of no use. I then got annoyed and threw the dough in disgust back into the vessel. The next moment I noticed some movement behind me. When I turned round I saw, to my consternation, Sri Bhagavan standing behind me and watching my efforts to make *vadai*. I was naturally agitated but he said quietly, "It doesn't matter. You have added too much water while grinding the black gram. Now make round balls of the dough and fry them. They will then be *bondas!*" I did accordingly.

When the *bondas* were served to the devotees at breakfast, as usual, Ramaswami Iyer said to me angrily, "Look here. Did I not ask you to prepare *vadai*? Then why have you made *bondas*?"

I was afraid to say anything and so merely looked at Sri Bhagavan who immediately turned to Ramaswami Iyer and said, "What does it matter? If the cakes are flat and circular they are *vadais*, if spherical, *bondas*. The stuff is the same and the taste is the same. Only names and forms are different. Eat the *prasadam* (food offered to a deity) and don't make a fuss." Everyone was astonished at the ready and apt reply of Sri Bhagavan. Ramaswami Iyer could not contain his joy! He exclaimed, "Wonderful, Wonderful!" Later in the day, when he saw me, he said, "I say, you are a lucky fellow. Sri Bhagavan himself is supporting you."

The world consists of names and forms. These are naturally many, but what lies behind them is one and the same. Names and forms are not real although we think that they are. Brahman which underlies them is real, but we forget it. What wisdom lay in Sri Bhagavan's words!

ɔଓ ଔ

# HOW I CAME TO THE MAHARSHI

## I

## Swami Paresananda

*Major General V. N. Parameswaran Pillai, O.B.E.,
retired from service as G.O.C., Travancore-Cochin State Forces
in the year 1950. Even while in service he had a deeply religious
bent of mind and he used to visit holy places and personages.
After retirement he made a pilgrimage to all holy places in
India and to Kailas-Manasarovar. He was initiated by Sri
Sivanandaji Maharaj of Rishikesh when he visited Trivandrum
in 1950. Sri Swami Purushottamanandaji Maharaj of Vasistha
Guha gave him sannyasa diksha in 1958. Since then he is
known as Swami Paresananda. He had his own Ashram at
Kanyakumari, Neyyathinkaray and Trivandrum.*

IT WAS in the year 1936 that I had the good fortune of having
*darshan* of Sri Bhagavan. I had heard about him before, and
was longing to go to Tiruvannamalai but the opportunity never
came till then. This is how it came about.

I was then a Captain in the Travancore State Forces and an
A.D.C. to His Highness the Maharaja. His Highness and the

Royal Mother had been to Madras from where they paid a visit to Sri Ramanasramam on the counsel of the Dewan, Sir C. P. Ramaswami Iyer, who was a devotee of Sri Ramana Bhagavan. I came to know of this when Their Highnesses returned to Trivandrum and was wondering whether it was not my bad luck that I was not taken as A.D.C. on that tour. In the meantime, one morning, my friend Sri I. S. Narayana Pillai, the Controller of Stationery, who was a devotee of Maharshi, informed me over the phone that he was starting for Sri Ramanasramam the next day and asked whether I would like to join him. It was his general practice to inform me whenever he went to some place of pilgrimage and I had accompanied him to many places. But this time I was not confident of getting permission from His Highness at such short notice and I replied that I would not be able to go with him.

Mysterious indeed are the ways of Bhagavan! A few hours later, when I reported for duty at the Palace, His Highness said, of his own accord, that if I also wanted to visit Sri Ramanasramam I could go. Yes, His Highness knew very well that I was fond of visiting religious places and saints. This sudden and unexpected permission made me speechless for a few seconds. I felt it was all due to Bhagavan's grace.

Sri I. S. and I reached the Ashram the second day. My companion was a frequent visitor, so everyone knew him. He introduced me to the *Sarvadhikari,* Sri Niranjanananda Swami who made arrangements for our stay. Then we proceeded to the hall for Sri Bhagavan's *darshan.* Bhagavan was reclining on a couch, turning to one side. The hall was almost full with visitors from various parts of the country and from the west. As we entered the hall, the scene brought to my memory, *slokas* from *Dakshinamurti Stotra.* I felt Dakshinamurti Himself was reclining on the couch. I. S. took me to a vantage point, sitting where we could see the Maharshi without any obstruction. Bhagavan noticed us. After a while he sat up and beckoned me. We did not know whom he was summoning and, as I was a stranger, my companion thought he was being called and he got up. Bhagavan signalled ' No '. Others enquired whether this or that person was meant by pointing to some persons sitting nearby but the answer was in the negative.

At last I was pointed out and Maharshi nodded assent. Everybody was surprised and became curious about me. I was also surprised. I approached him immediately, placed the flowers and fruits I had brought, and prostrated before him. He beckoned me to come nearer and gazed at me for a while and smiled. Then he told his attendant "Bring that book." It was brought and Maharshi presented it to me. It was a Malayalam translation of Maharshi's Tamil work, *Gitasaram*. I was overwhelmed with joy and devotion. After a few seconds Maharshi took the book from me, made some corrections in his own hand and then handed it back to me touching my hand, I considered myself highly blessed to receive Maharshi's Grace in this manner.

Then it was time for the midday meal. We were also invited; so we entered the dining hall. Maharshi asked me to sit in the opposite row, just facing him and I did so. While eating, he enquired tenderly, "How is the preparation?" and so on. I replied that everything was very nice. Again he said, "Take enough rice, curry, etc. Eat slowly", and so on, and asked the servers to serve me more curry etc. Throughout he was talking to me only in the dining hall and this made others wonder who this favoured one might be. As for me, I had had various such experiences before and I felt that it was all due to some merit accumulated in past lives. "Omnipresent and Omniscient as he is, Maharshi understands the heart of every one", this belief of mine was confirmed.

My friend I. S. was a regular visitor to the Ashram but Maharshi had never spoken to him. When I received such favours from him, it was natural for I. S. to feel that there was something lacking in him. Maharshi could easily understand this. The same day he presented a book to I. S. also and made him feel deeply gratified.

More than thirty-seven years have elapsed but the whole thing is still green in my memory. And the book that Maharshi gave me, corrected in his own hand, is still with me—I keep it as a treasure.

# II

## Sunyata

*Sunya Baba — Emmanual Sorensen in his* purvashrama — *refers to himself always in the third person in the article.*

IT WAS IN THE YEAR 1929 that Poet Rabindranath Tagore and his secretaries (Arya Nikam and Amiya Chakravarti) met him and I befriended him at Dartington Hall in Devonshire, England. And it was the Poet's casual invitation to the simple, 'uneducated' gardener to come to Bharat 'to teach Silence' to the ebullient Bengalis, which called him here. He discerned in the simpleton's Being a quality of Sunya-Santi-Silence and intuitive awareness which was felt to be congenial and appreciated in India. The invitation gave the sadhu-type the needed push or pull, to venture forth simply and solitarily into India, and the proposed 3 or 4 months' stay stretched into 45 years of Himalayan ananda-grace. The solitary pilgrim in Consciousness had come ' Home'. In India he read the Vedas, the Upanishads and the writings of genuine Masters.

He heard of Sri Ramana Maharshi while in Kashmir and Tibet from Lamas, and later from Paul Brunton and Dr. W. Y. EvansWentz. After spending several years in the Himalayas and other sanctuaries, he came to Sri Ramana Maharshi in the year 1936 for the first time and was introduced to the Maharshi by Paul Brunton. He also came three times or more later at a few years' intervals. He had no problem, no disease, and no quest and so asked no questions. Maharshi, however, did ask him some questions which he has now forgotten.

But the first *darshan* of the Maharshi remains an unforgettable experience, especially Sri Ramana's casual, as it were, statement ' We are always aware'; and this made a most powerful impact on him. It resounded in his consciousness like a chime and continued to linger in his memory like a mantra or an echo of Sri Arunachala or Dakshinamurti. He also remembers some passages mentioned from the Bible: the phrase, 'I AM THAT I AM', 'Be Still and know that I am God', 'Know ye not that you are Gods?' and the words Jesus exchanged with Nicodemus.

He found Ramana Maharshi's was pure advaita-experience, and his chief language, radiant Silence, to which only mature souls familiar with solitude could easily respond. When Ramana was questioned by officious officials and was later asked if it had tired him, he said: "No; I did not use my mind". He was mind-free and ego-free.

As for Sunya, there was from babyhood no sense of guilt, no sin-complex and no ego-pitiful grievance against What Is. Very little friction, imposition or conditioning, and so no ego-importance. Affectionate detachment from forms and things, is natural in the conscious awareness that there is no real division, no real detachment in the Reality we ever are, ego-free and death-free. There is no ambition to 'become' this or that and no reaching out for power or self-possessions, security. Yet, there is intuitive Light-awareness, a flair for essence, wholeness and esoteric grace-awareness; a secure contentment in the fundamental all-Rightness of things and happenings as Siva Lila, Self-interplay.

# III

## Satya Narayan Tandon

IT WAS AT THE END OF 1944 that I first heard about Bhagavan Ramana Maharshi. I was sitting with a religious teacher, when a visitor said: "Maharshi is Mount Everest and others mere hillocks." Since then I had a persistent urge to have darshan of Sri Bhagavan.

In the summer of 1946, when I was sitting in the presence of Paramsant Mahatma Raghuber Dayal, a Sufi saint, a fellow-devotee who had been to Tiruvannamalai began to speak about Sri Bhagavan, the Ashram and his experiences during his stay there. Chachaji, (as we used to call the saint) who had listened attentively to his devotee's narration, spoke very highly about Sri Bhagavan. This only strengthened my desire to have his *darshan*.

But I did not get the opportunity for it — one hindrance or another always came in my way.

Early in April 1950, when I was planning to go to Arunachala, my younger brother, Sri Jagatnarayan, told me that he along with a friend was to leave for Tiruvannamalai the same evening. To me this was a bolt from the blue, as we both could not leave the station simultaneously. I could not speak out my mind, and he left for Tiruvannamalai. He was fortunate to have Sri Bhagavan's *darshan* — standing in a queue. He stayed there for a few days and on the return journey somewhere near Nagpur, got the information that Sri Bhagavan had shed the body.

My younger brother again went to Sri Ramanasramam in 1956. On hearing from him about the Ashram and his experiences there, the longing to visit the Shrine was aroused afresh.

It was late in 1957 at the insistence of my wife, that my longing to visit the shrine of Sri Ramana Maharshi was fulfilled.

Since 1957, Sri Bhagavan has been graciously pleased to call us to his Shrine of Grace practically every year.

An accident that occurred at Allahabad Railway station on the morning of January 23, 1972 is worth recording.

With my younger son, his wife and one of my grandsons, I was coming back to Kanpur from Allahabad by Howrah-Kalka Mail. After locating our berths, I was talking on the platform with people who had come to see us off. I could not hear the whistle of the electric engine, and the train began to move. I caught hold of the handle of the compartment to get into it. But I lost the grip and fell on the track. In the meantime the train had gathered momentum. When my son, who was at the other door of the compartment, enquired about me, a fellow-passenger told him that he saw an old man falling down while trying to get into the compartment. My son immediately pulled the chain, but the train stopped only two furlongs away.

As soon as I fell on the track, I saw the face of Sri Bhagavan repeating like a *mantra*, "Don't lift the head." Where I was on the track I cannot say. But I saw the wheels moving faster and faster.

When the entire train had moved beyond the place where I was, I got up though my head and left eye-brow were badly wounded, so much so that my woollen coat had become drenched. The guard who was in charge of the train said that eight bogeys had passed over me and that it was a miracle that I had escaped death. It was all his benign Grace that he saved this body, for what purpose is known to him only. For the first few days after the wounds had been stitched and I was in great agony and pain, I was kept under sedation but I felt Sri Bhagavan sitting by my side and at times moving his hands over the wounds that had been stitched.

My cap and spectacles that had fallen on the track were all received by my people without any damage whatsoever. The same glasses and the same frame I used for years thereafter.

May this head remain at his Lotus feet for the rest of my days on earth.

ॐ ॐ

# AWARENESS ABSOLUTE

## Visvanatha Swami

IT WAS AT Skandasramam on Arunachala that I first met
Bhagavan Ramana (in January 1921). He was standing on
the open space in front of the Ashram building facing the
entrance as I approached. The very sight of him was thrilling;
something very subtle, seemingly with its centre in that body,
shone forth unlimited engulfing everything else. Needless to
say I felt swallowed up by it. I stayed for a week with Bhagavan
in that atmosphere of utter purity and serenity. I heard from
him how he came to Arunachala, irresistibly attracted and swept
off his feet by a tremendous benevolent force; how he was one
with it deep down within his heart almost oblivious of his body
and surroundings; and how only later on he gradually regained
the use of his senses and mind and was able to look about and
commune with others when they approached him.

Subsequently too, when I had come to Bhagavan for good,
the effect of his proximity continued the same way and I may
say that there was no necessity for any *sadhana* in particular on
my part. Along with a few other inmates I had my share in the
work of the Ashram in the elevating company of Bhagavan and
I studied his few works, devotional and philosophical, and heard
his replies to various questions put by visitors. But the most
important thing was the mere Presence, the spiritually uplifting

company of Bhagavan. As Bhagavan says in the *Supplement to the Reality in Forty Verses*: "If one associates with Sages, where is the need for any other rigorous *sadhana*? No one looks for a fan when there is the pleasant southern breeze."

The climax of my spiritual experience in the proximity of Bhagavan was during his 'last' moments. As I stood in that small room along with a very few others, everything became shadow enveloped by one indivisible Pure Awareness, the one and only ever-present Reality. And so there was not the least feeling of any separation from Bhagavan or the least vestige of sorrow on that account. Not only that, there was a positive ecstasy and elation of spirit which is nothing but the Natural State of the Self.

All those who approached Bhagavan with spiritual earnestness have had this experience of direct contact with the Divine at the very first sight of Bhagavan. Ganapati Muni, the great poet and *tapaswin*, saw an adept (a *Siddha Purusha*, a Perfect Being) in Bhagavan, the moment he first beheld him by chance on the Hill in the Ashram of Jataiswami. The scholar became a disciple. Venkataramanier of Satyamangalam saw Bhagavan as a clear manifestation of the all-pervading Supreme Self and sang his five superb Hymns in Praise of Ramana. Humphreys saw Bhagavan as a glowing centre of Divine Radiance. Achyuta Dasa, Narayana Guru and so many others seeing Bhagavan recognised his unique spiritual greatness. Pascaline Mallet, a French lady, who stayed with Bhagavan for a few months sang in a poem in praise of Bhagavan: "One Light, One Life, One Love, shining through Thee, we see." And Grant Duff (Douglas Ainslee), the cultured scholar and poet, says in his preface to Bhagavan's *Five Hymns to Arunachala:* "I was in direct contact with one who had passed beyond the boundaries of the senses and was merged in the Absolute Self. I do not need any proof of the divinity of Ramana Maharshi, just as I do not need any to prove the existence of the Sun."

What is the secret behind the common experience of Divine Glory which so many intelligent devotees have had in the presence of Bhagavan? Here is the answer given by Ganapati Muni in his remarkable hymn of *Forty Verses in Praise of Bhagavan*: "Bow down to the holy Guru Ramana who reaching the hidden source of the ego within has effaced all differentiation and shines forth as the One Self of all beings with various mental propensities and who is resplendent as the One Reality transcending the body and the entire world-manifestation." "I bow to Sri Ramana, the Great Teacher, the remover of all sorrow, who established in the Eternal Abode of Pure Awareness dispels the ignorance of earnest seekers, who though seeing and moving within the world stands as the Supreme Being transcending it."

Whatever is seen is non-self and the Seer alone is the unchanging Self. When we take to Self-enquiry holding on to this fundamental principle of Vedanta, the physical body, the life-current operating in it and the mind are eliminated as non-self. Even the intellect, the highest known principle in man with its reasoning faculty, has to be discarded as non-self as it is only the faculty of one behind it, claiming it as his. Who is he? He cannot stand by himself and so he disappears. What then remains as the source of the elusive I-sense in us is the ultimate Self, which is ever there as the Ground of all that appears and disappears, of all perception in the waking and dream states and non-perception of anything in deep sleep.

Though the truth of the ultimate Self is explained within a few steps like this, the enveloping power of a mysterious force of darkness known as *avarana* in Vedanta is such that it gets eradicated only after a vigilant self-enquiry constantly carried on. The inherent tendencies *(vasanas)* of the mind based on a phantom ego get annihilated only after a continuous earnest attempt to abide at the Heart, the Source. So, Sankara says in his *Vivekachudamani* that liberation *(mukti)* is nothing but the complete eradication of the ego with all its *vasanas*. Bhagavan says in his song on Atma Vidya that Grace is needed for the dawn of *jnana* as well as earnest aspiration and devotion on the part of the seeker to deserve it. When earnest effort and Grace meet, then there is the achievement of the highest spiritual aspiration of man, viz., spontaneous inherence in the ever-present Self.

The Self is Pure Awareness, unalloyed Awareness itself, whereas the mind is awareness of this and that. The mind cannot stand for a moment without an object, because it is by its very nature a subject-object phenomenon. It disappears when it is divested of objects, unable to stand by itself. And there, the Self, the one indivisible absolute Awareness shines for ever as stated in *Sri Ramana Gita* (Ch. vii, v.5): "When the ego which is but a phantom of the Self totally disappears, what remains is the real Self alone in all its plenitude and perfection." This is *jnana* and this is *mukti* (liberation).

For one established in it thus, the subject-object phenomena may appear and disappear but he will remain for ever unsullied as Pure Awareness, since nothing has any existence apart from it. This is known as *Tanmaya Nishta*. Being the Self is Awareness of the Self.

From a relative standpoint, the proximity of such a Sage, normally established in the Self under all circumstances of life, serves as an eye-opener for those in the clutches of delusion and as an invaluable aid supporting them in their spiritual quest.

The operation of the Spiritual Force of such enlightened Ones is not limited to the lifetime of their physical body. It continues for ever and those who think of them, surrender themselves to them, study their life and teachings and try to follow them do get into the ambit of their Grace, non-different from Supreme Divine Grace. This is the experience of so many spiritual aspirants who had not met Bhagavan during his lifetime but devoted themselves to him on hearing of him or coming to know of him somehow or other. The enlightened Ones who are themselves timeless belong to all time and by their very nature shed light on the path of seekers and help them in ever so many ways.

Ultimately one sees that one has no existence apart from Pure Awareness, that there is no world apart from it and that there is no other God than Pure Awareness. Blissful Awareness is the sole Reality. Manifestation as the Many is nothing but its Lila. Every one, in manifestation, has to play his part knowing at heart that it is all nothing but *Lila*, the only Reality being Absolute Blissful Awareness.

రు శు

# SRI BHAGAVAN'S BODILY HEALTH

## K. Lakshmana Sarma

AN INEVITABLE CONSEQUENCE of Bhagavan's state as a *jivan mukta,* permanently established in the egoless State, was that he could not claim any rights, even the right to choose what shall be done or not done to his body, because from his point of view, that body was not his. Also, he was so full of compassion, that he could not bear to hurt anyone's feelings. Anyone that came to him offering edibles or medicine, was sure of its being accepted, though he did not want it. Once he said, "Nature cure is right. But...." And he did not complete the sentence.

Yet he showed his real view of drugs by implication. When a quantity of a drug had to be taken for a certain period, he would take only one dose and would never take a second; that is, he would not follow the prescription as one who believed in the goodness of the drug would do, so as to benefit by it.

The same was the case when an operation was proposed. He submitted to the operation only to please the person who wanted to do him good.

On the last occasion, when a number of doctors and surgeons who came from Madras wanted to operate on him to remove the cancer he was having, he first very gently suggested that it was not necessary. He did that because he knew the future, that the end was near. The doctors did not take the hint. They insisted on operating and hence Sri Bhagavan submitted to the operation without an anaesthetic. The operation lasted for nearly three hours and produced a severe shock, from which the body never recovered.

When all these medical efforts had failed, a number of devotees came to him and prayed to him to use his spiritual powers to heal the disease. Bhagavan replied, "I did not want any treatment. It was you that wanted it." After a brief pause he added, "In two more days it will become all right". What he meant was that the end would come then. And it came exactly as he said.

ॐ

# TREATMENT TO SRI BHAGAVAN – AN ACCOUNT

## Dr. Shankar Rao

*Dr.Shankar Rao, a retired D. M. O., who was attending on Sri Maharshi almost from the start of his illness, details in this article an intimate and vivid picture of the Maharshi's ailment and the way he bore with it.*

TO HAVE SERVED Bhagavan Sri Ramana Maharshi as a doctor for over a year is no ordinary privilege and no ordinary experience. It was an education of the highest type, a training of a unique character. It provided me with vivid glimpses into the human as well as the superhuman and godlike personality of Sri Maharshi.

For one whole year I watched the ailment sapping the strength and vitality of the physical frame of Sri Maharshi with cruel success. It failed to affect his detachment and composure and I found for the first time that this disease with its brood of pain and suffering had somehow met with an ignominious defeat. This will be borne out in the following account of the history of the ailment which culminated in the Maharshi shaking off the mortal sheath.

I first came to Sri Ramanashram in the second week of December, 1948. At that time Sri Bhagavan had a small nodule under the skin behind the elbow about the size of a split pea. When I asked him about it he said that it might have been due to a fall he had some three months back. On pressing, it used to be painful. Within a month it grew to the size of a small marble. Sri Bhagavan used to feel pain whenever he put his elbow on any hard surface and so I suggested its removal. It was removed on 9th February 1949. The wound completely healed up during the course of a week.

In the first week of March, it was again noticed to be growing. About the middle of March, Dr. Raghavachari of Madras came with his assistants and removed it completely, together with a good deal of surrounding tissues and also the skin over it. A microscopic examination revealed that it was a sarcoma.

Sarcoma is a malignant tumour of the flesh which occurs generally in young people, while older ones get cancers which are growths from the skin or mucous membranes. These malignant tumours are not enclosed in sheaths or capsules like simple tumours. Even small microscopic cells anywhere in the tissues surrounding the tumour could start to grow into another tumour. Some cells may be carried through the blood vessels to other parts of the body and produce similar secondary tumours.

The wound, after the second operation, did not heal and after a few days, a new growth appeared and this started bleeding profusely. Doctors and radiologists came from Madras and applied radium to afford temporary relief. They advised that amputation of the limb, a couple of inches above the tumour alone could cure the disease. The consensus of opinion amongst the devotees of Sri Bhagavan was against amputation. Sri

Bhagavan also said that it was not necessary. The idea of amputation was given up.

The tumour growth subsided a little as a result of radium treatment but in July 1949 it again began to grow. Some of the devotees wished that ayurvedic treatment should be tried and a local ayurvedic physician started treatment. Sri Bhagavan's health deteriorated, sepsis set in and the tumour continued to grow very rapidly.

Surgeons from Madras were again requested to come. They advised an operation as the only remedy and the tumour together with the white area of tissues all around were removed with a diathermic knife. Radium was then applied. This was on 14th August.

The result appeared to be very favourable in as much as no tumour growth appeared for three months and even scrapings taken from the raw surface of the wound were reported to be negative. Early in December 1949 however, there was a suspicion of a small nodule appearing in the middle of the arm, several inches away from the site of the original tumour growth. Then again doctors from Madras came and having diagnosed it as a secondary growth and that too a very small one, they expected to remove it easily.

On 19th December the growth was operated on but when the deeper tissues were cut into, for removing the tumour, it was found that the growth had spread deep into the muscles. A much larger operation became necessary and in spite of this, the surgeons felt that the chances of recurrence could not be ruled out.

As the surgeons had given up hope of a cure, homeopathy was tried. By about the middle of February, the tumour again started growing on the upper end of the operation wound and as the homeopath who was treating Sri Bhagavan was unable to prevent recurrence, an ayurvedic physician from Malabar was sent for and he started treatment. This too having been unsuccessful, Kaviraj Jogendranath Sastry from Calcutta was invited by one of the devotees to treat Sri Bhagavan. During all this period the general health of Sri Bhagavan continued to deteriorate and the tumour growth increased rapidly.

By about the 2nd of April I felt that the end was near. On the night of Sunday the 9th of April the pulse became very feeble and gradual deterioration of the functions of the heart brought about exhaustion. Sri Bhagavan who, until that day, had been able to walk to the adjoining bathroom could not do so and was confined to bed.

Since February the blood pressure of Sri Bhagavan started dropping. A fortnight before the end it was 88/48, the lowest point reached being 66/36. The expected end came at 8.47 pm on 14th April.

Sri Bhagavan's attitude towards his body was one of complete detachment. Disease and pain left no impression on his mind. If he allowed himself to be treated for the ailment, it was more because his devotees wanted it than because he desired relief. His attitude was always supreme indifference to bodily ailments.

So he was an ideal patient implicitly undergoing any treatment that was decided upon by his devotees. Whenever he allowed any change in treatment his only concern was that there should be an agreement amongst his devotees about which particular type of treatment should be given a trial. As far as he personally was concerned, he did not care.

To everyone who was by his side, the way in which he bore with pain, which was at times of an extremely excruciating nature, without even showing the signs of suffering on his face, was a wonder. On one occasion during the later stages of the ailment when he was having shooting pains down his limb, a gentlemen who had come for his *darshan* bowed down and said that he was leaving Tiruvannamalai. Sri Bhagavan gave him his usual gracious look and smile as if there was nothing wrong with him at the time. And it was only after the gentleman left that Sri Bhagavan admitted that the pain was severe and allowed himself to be treated for it.

The tumour in the later stages of his illness grew to such proportions that even medical men who were used to those sights were shocked when they saw it. When it was being dressed, Sri Bhagavan used to look at it and often make jokes about it. He even helped the doctors to adjust the bandage.

On one occasion when the skin around the tumour was being cleaned with rectified spirit, some of it bathed the rest of the arm and fell on the body also. Sri Bhagavan jokingly said that he was having a spirit bath and quoted the last stanza of *Atma Bodha* by Sri Shankaracharya. It was not only a joke but also carried with it a profound spiritual teaching.

One night when there was heavy bleeding from the tumour as it was being dressed, two or three *bhaktas* couldn't conceal their emotion. He looked at them and said, "Where will I go? And where can I go?" And whenever he said 'I', with emphasis, he always meant the *Atman*.

Some time ago when treating the tumour it was suggested that Sri Bhagavan should have a sun bath and the tumour was exposed to the sun for a few minutes. To prevent flies, some incense was put in an oven and placed just below the chair upon which he sat. Sri Bhagavan jokingly said that we were offering worship to the tumour to go away by burning incense and waving lights (*dhoopam* and *deepam*) before it.

One of my friends took photographs of Sri Bhagavan one afternoon. During the night when we both went together and I was dressing the wound, Sri Bhagavan referred to the photos and gave a profound spiritual discourse using the science of photography as an illustration. Said Sri Bhagavan,

"When taking a picture the silver salts are coated over a film in the dark and when the film is exposed in the camera, you get an impression caused by light outside. If the film is exposed to light before you put it in the camera there can be no impression on it. So is it with our *jiva*. When it is still in darkness, impression can be made on it by the little light that leaks in. But when the light of knowledge has already flooded it, there is no impression of external objects to be obtained." In a similar fashion, he used to entertain his medical attendants with jokes interspersed with profound spiritual education.

Throughout the period of illness, his desire not to embarrass his medical attendants in whatever system of medicine they belonged, resulted in a perfect code of medical etiquette that could not be excelled. When he was having treatment of a particular system of medicine such as ayurveda or homeopathy, if any one suggested a remedy for the intense pain he was having, he would always refer him to the doctor that was in attendance and ask him to get his consent. On one occasion when the surgeons who operated on him had confessed that nothing short of an amputation could cure Sri Bhagavan, a devotee of many years' standing, brought an eminent physician of another system of medicine. This gentleman saw Sri Bhagavan and had a talk with him. Sri Bhagavan received him with his usual gracious smile and the new physician believed that Sri Bhagavan wished him to treat him.

It was characteristic of Sri Bhagavan — and this was observed by many of his devotees — that when each individual went to him, he returned with a feeling that the Master had poured his grace on him alone and that he was the most loved amongst his devotees! I knew this and therefore took this physician to Sri Bhagavan and asked him to obtain his consent for the treatment. Sri Bhagavan smiled at this and said, "Do you know doctor so and so who is now treating me? Have you had a talk with him and what did he say?" The gentleman was nonplussed and had to go.

To watch Sri Bhagavan and listen even to his day-to-day talk was an education to those who were near him. There was no need to read books on religion or philosophy. His whole philosophy and the philosophy of ages were in Sri Bhagavan's life. For his life was an exposition of the highest philosophy. He did not lecture. He did not write books for the edification of learned scholars outside but by living the life of perfection, he gave to those that came in contact with him, a greater education than any books could provide. With the passing of the greatest spiritual personality of modern times, the world has lost a living teacher, a guru in its highest sense.

ॐ ॐ

# THE END WAS PEACEFUL

## Eye-witness Account of a Medical Officer Who Attended on Sri Maharshi

### Lt. Col. P.V. Karamchandani

*How Shri Maharshi responded with spontaneous quickness to sincere requests and prayers, even during his last moments, is here detailed by a reputed physician who skethes the sombre yet touchingly majestic setting of the Master's mahanirvana.*

THE EXTRAORDINARY PRIVILEGE of attending on Bhagavan Sri Maharshi during the last two months came to me rather unexpectedly and without any planning on my part.

About fifteen years ago while I was working in Trichy, a friend from North India wrote to me asking particulars about Tiruvannamalai and Sri Ramana Maharshi. I wrote back saying that I had neither seen nor heard about the town and the sage and that I was interested in neither.

In December last year I was posted to North Arcot and very soon after, a medical officer came to me, invited me to visit the hospital at Tiruvannamalai and also added that the occasion could be availed of to see Sri Ramana Maharshi. Though the casual mention of Tiruvannamalai evoked memories of my friend's query, I had no impelling urge to go to the district town.

Official work however, took me to Tiruvannamalai after some months. When my inspection work was over, it was suggested to me that I could pay a visit to the Ashram. I agreed. I went to the Ashram and there saw Sri Bhagavan.

Before I saw Sri Maharshi, I had been told that he was four times operated on, for sarcoma. When I examined him, I found a small ulcer in his arm above the elbow. At the upper end of the ulcer there was a swelling. I couldn't be certain as to whether this was the tumour growth coming up again after the operation or whether it was ordinary inflammation. I suggested penicillin to eliminate this doubt. Penicillin was not given and in course of time it proved to be a tumour growth.

I was called again to Tiruvannamalai only after six weeks. When I saw Sri Bhagavan this time, I found a big growth almost covering the upper left arm except for a two inch space in front. This growth was bleeding and losing serum, thereby directly depleting the system of bodily fluids. Added to this there was pain, which was exhausting the body. More than haemorrhage and loss of serum, pain was the distressing feature.

The variety of tumour that Sri Bhagavan had was spindle shaped sarcoma, probably arising from the sheath of the ulnar nerve. This is a very painful tumour with its speciality of shooting pain. In medical language we call it lacinating pain but Sri Bhagavan described it as something like insects creeping up and down the arm! He bore with this pain as though the body did not belong to him. Whenever I asked him whether there was pain, Sri Bhagavan said that it was nothing.

Within this period I came again and found the tumour furiously growing, draining the system fast and also arousing some sensation of pain in the impregnable and imperturbable personality of Sri Bhagavan. I could only illustrate this by one tiny incident. A few days before Sri Bhagavan's departure someone touched the cloth on the tumour and there appeared an expression of pain on his face. The attendant who touched the cloth said that he touched only the cloth on the tumour and not the tumour itself. To which Sri Bhagavan replied that the cloth bore the weight of mountains!

I came to see Sri Bhagavan at about midnight on the 13th instant. I found him resting with closed eyes. When he opened them, he asked all the attendants to clear out of the room. He repeated this half a dozen times and this was interpreted as delirium. But I examined him and found him to be fully conscious, and not at all delirious. I asked the attendants to obey Sri Bhagavan's instructions by going out of the room. Throughout the night I sat with him. There was respiratory embarrassment (Cheyne Stoke breathing as we call it). Pain was very intense because even the least movement brought forth evidence of pain.

I left in the morning and came back in the evening, just two hours before Sri Bhagavan's last breath. This privilege of being by his side at that time was something which I prayed for but which I little expected. When I entered his room, Sri Bhagavan's eyes were closed. He was propped up on his bed and breathing was very hard. The lips were parched and I gave him some drops of water. I thought that a little fruit juice would be better. I asked him, "Bhagavan, shall I give you some orange juice?" I repeated the question twice and each time Sri Bhagavan shook his head to mean 'no'.

Then a strange thing happened. I stood beside him prayerfully repeating the question within my mind. Suddenly, Sri Maharshi nodded his head to mean 'yes' and opened his mouth. I gave him three teaspoons of juice. Each time he opened his mouth and swallowed the juice. This was the last nourishment that Sri Bhagavan had. This was at about 7.45 pm.

At ten minutes to eight, Sri Maharshi's pulse was still perceptible. A big crowd of devotees was sorrowfully waiting outside expecting and fearing that the last breath would be taken at any minute. I felt that it was not a question of minutes and to relieve the prevailing tension, a bulletin was issued to the effect that there was no immediate danger to life. This relieved the assembled devotees a little. At twenty five minutes to nine, the pulse was still perceptible and the breathing was very hard and laborious. It was distressing beyond words to see that mighty personality suffering such pains. I asked within myself why such a great soul should undergo such agonies. Had he taken on himself the karma of others? If he should suffer such pains what about others? Could not Sri Bhagavan relieve himself of the pain? Thoughts like these weighed in my mind as I stood watching Sri Bhagavan.

As though to provide an answer to my suffering, the picture changed and changed suddenly. The pulse disappeared and breathing became slow and easy, a very unusual feature at such a time and stage. The breathing became slower and slower till it completely stopped at thirteen to nine. The last breath was as easy and slow as any other previous breath. We were able to decide the last breath only from the fact that there were no breaths after. The jerk, the struggle and the gasps that usually announce the last breath in the case of ordinary people were not there in the case of Sri Bhagavan.

And so slowly and smoothly Sri Bhagavan secured his release from his physical encasement. That was the end.

No. How could that be? Sri Bhagavan has no beginning and no end.

# ARADHANA DAY

## I

## Major Chadwick

*(These articles were written to commemorate Bhagavan's third* Aradhana*)*

ON MAY 11TH the Ashram celebrates Sri Bhagavan's third *Aradhana*, when one will be carried back to that momentous night three years ago when he passed. One can still see the tense crowds seated in rows under the veranda of the new hall, waiting, waiting, waiting till the last breath should be breathed and the one they all loved so much should once and for all relinquish his body. Most of us felt it would be a happy release. We prayed he might be spared any further suffering. The sickness and pain had been so long drawn out, it was an agony to watch the loved one being slowly wasted away by the malignant disease.

Doubtless he was a *jnani* and was beyond all suffering, he was dwelling in the bliss of the Self, but suffering there undoubtedly was, though he himself would have asked, "To whom is the suffering?" It is a mystery beyond my comprehension. Vaguely, I sense that if one is liberated, one is free from all pain as the Self is all bliss. Behind even suffering there must be a special bliss for such. It is only a surface appearance, though very real and painful for the onlooker.

Swami Ramathirtha used to say that when he had high fever he experienced the most ecstatic bliss during meditation, more so than when he was in normal health. At first people felt lost, they had relied too much on the personal form, though Bhagavan himself had repeatedly warned them, "You attach too much importance to this body."

Still it was only natural that this body should be missed, although as time went on, the loss became gradually less keen. His presence was felt so strongly in the Ashram, and daily the feeling of this actual presence grew. A visitor remarked to me lately, "One does not miss the presence of Bhagavan in the Ashram, he is there just as he was before." And this is true. He is there and he is surely working and the Ashram will grow in strength and renown as time goes on. There have been dark days since that night three years ago, but those days are now past. The Ashram takes on a new life. There is a new feeling in the air and the stagnation is over. The school has been revived and *pujas* are performed so carefully and enthusiastically that the whole place rings with the vibrations thus set up.

I went away never to return, but he brought me back. And now I thank him every day that I have been allowed to take part in this renaissance. It is thrilling to the core to feel it happening. One should have known that it was bound to be like this all the time. How could anything happen to the place he had sanctified with his presence for so long? The whole of India was blessed by his life, how much more so the place in which he made his home.

I have one piece of advice to offer to one and all. Do not believe the stories you hear about Sri Ramanasramam because you can always test the truth of such tales for yourself without relying on hearsay. It is very easy. Come and see for yourself. You will not be disappointed.

# II

## Mouni Sadhu

THREE YEARS AGO the sad news of the departure from the physical body of Bhagavan Sri Ramana Maharshi came to me and his other devotees scattered throughout the world. I do not wish to praise or compare the great Being at whose feet the Almighty allowed me to abide.

For how could we, from our lower level of consciousness, describe exactly this Being whose mission was to give us something of his infinite light? And for adequate assessing of his greatness, one must at least be on the same level of spiritual glory. All that I can do is try to convey, what I found in my own heart, when I received news of his departure.

The light from those luminous eyes of Sri Bhagavan, was for ever engraved on my memory when leaving the Ashram. And now the account of his death lies before me. Does it mean that those eyes cannot any more radiate their silent initiation? That the light of eternity has been really extinguished? That would be ridiculous, I know this light is not a material one, though it was conveyed through a material body. This is a mystery but not a paradox. I found in my heart no urge to discover that mystery through the mind. I feel that the fact was so, even though unexplainable by the thinking process. So his death did not deprive me of his reality.

I was sitting quietly, as in preparation for meditation, but this time, the usual process was changed. Perhaps he saw that the human heart, not yet free from all its weaknesses, needs sometimes some consolation. And then, instead of a void, the well known and beloved picture arose before me.

There were most mysterious and inspiring evenings at the Ashram, when the beautiful hymn "In praise of the Lord of the Universe" (*Five hymns on Arunachala*) was sung in the hall. Sri Bhagavan evidently loved the hymn, for there would appear a peculiar expression of other than human beatitude and delight on his face. I felt that the hearts of those who were present in that blissful hour of evening contemplation were deeply attuned to it. Perhaps his penetrating inner sight saw the beneficial process in it, and his silent blessing was the answer. How can we fathom what is unfathomable? And now I experienced once again, as with all those others who were present, the same beautiful melody heard before with my outer ears. It was as if I reviewed a film. There was no sadness any more. Could it be otherwise? The true legacy of the Master could never be less than joy this sublime and silent joy of Being, untroubled by the waves of the surrounding illusory world or *maya*. This was his peace which he bequeathed to us.

Later came letters from devotees from other continents. My distant friends gave their own accounts of how the tragic news affected them. They tried their best to console themselves and me, saying that the physical departure of the Master could not break our spiritual link with him. And yet the ink in the last paragraphs of such letters was often blurred as from fallen tears.

It is said that love was the force that created the Universe. Perhaps it is. But to me the force of such unselfish love as his, is just that power that purifies our hearts, when all other methods prove useless. No occult training nor any other method can give the disciple the true peace which the Master gives.

Sri Maharshi was a centre of love such as this, to his disciples. He left us his love and where else in the world could be found a purifying power such as this to bring peace to our hearts?

The anniversaries of the *mahasamadhi* of Sri Bhagavan will come one after another and one year will see the last one for me on this earth. But at the last moment he will be with me, as with every one of you who knew him, if you keep to the end, his legacy of love.

CB ഓ

# BHAGAVAN IS EVERYWHERE

## S.G. Devaraj

I HAD SEEN Bhagavan's pictures and heard about him, but was not particularly drawn to him until 1975. One afternoon in September of that year in a busy street in an American city, I saw a man walking ahead of me with a bag on his back on which the Sankskrit word *AUM* was embroidered. Prompted to talk to this man, I invited him to have a cup of tea in a nearby restaurant. I asked him how it happened that his bag bore the Sanskrit word *AUM*. He opened the bag and took out the book *Talks with Sri Ramana Maharshi* and a few other books about the Maharshi. We talked for a while and this north American told me, "I was an ordinary person like the rest here in this country. I had a job and a good income, a car and friends and relatives. Everything was OK but I was worried about my possessions being stolen and I had to make sure that my apartment was properly locked. I was worried all the time about losing my possessions. Somehow I got some books about Bhagavan and read them and then things started changing. Now this bag is all I have. I do not have a place I call mine. I do not have a job. If I need money I work for a few hours or for a day and what I earn could get a meal with no questions asked. All the time I spend reading these books about Bhagavan. I keep reading them again and again, but each time I learn something new."

It was this strange encounter with an unknown person in a city far away from Arunachala, who gave up all his possessions except the bag on his back, that prompted me to make a trip to Bhagavan's Ashram. We reached the Ashram around 3p.m. on the 25th anniversary of his *mahanirvana*. Putting our bedding and luggage in a room and getting a copy of the Ashram schedule, we went up the Hill to Skandashram, drank the spring water, spent a few minutes in the room there and returned in time for the evening meal at the Ashram. During our 1979 visit, my daughter, looking at Bhagavan's picture in the old meditation hall and said to her mother, "Amma, I see light in those eyes". In April of 1982, I was planning to visit India to bring my family back to the US to join me. In the same city where I met the strange person who gave up all his possessions except the bag on his back, circumstances brought me into contact with another American just a couple of days before I was to start my trip to India. My new friend, learning of my trip to India, wanted me to go to Tiruvannamalai and meet his friends (whom he named) in the Ashram!

This encounter with a total stranger was for me a blessing and a welcome to this home by Bhagavan Himself. Since the first trip in 1976, Sri Bhagavan made it possible for me to come to his feet no less than six times. Not only that, he made it possible for me to go to Madurai and spend some time in the spot where he had his realisation. What I was at the time of my first trip and what I am now, only I know and he knows. At present I am far, far away, physically, but again and again he makes his presence felt in innumerable ways. HE IS EVERYWHERE.

# BHAGAVAN SRI RAMANA IS PERSONALLY PRESENT HERE

## Swatantra

*(Sri Bhagavan is very much alive! His continued Presence at Sri Ramanasramam is sure to be felt by sincere seekers of Truth, stresses the author of this article.)*

BHAGAVAN SRI RAMANA is personally present here. To demand proof is like wanting proof that the sun is shining overhead. His presence is known or 'seen' by those with eyes to see. For others even a positive proof would be useless.

If a few phenomenal incidents are cited to prove his personal presence here, the logical mind may well dismiss them all as too fantastic or merely imagination. A man of faith could accept the facts on hearing them but would that instill conviction of Sri Ramana's presence as a living reality?

For those who come to visit Sri Ramanasramam, I would like to offer my advice. Please do not come like a tourist merely with an idea that you are going to sight — see an Ashram. Even if it bears the name of one of the greatest *Rishis* of modern times. Don't go through the ritual of offering prayers and *puja* at various shrines, receiving *prasadam* and *vibhuti* only to go back satisfied that you have 'done' with another holy place.

Of course, visiting holy places does have great effect, but that in itself is not enough. It may be enough for the uninitiated, but seekers of the Truth require a sense of holy presence, such as can be experienced at Sri Ramanasramam. It is a fact that Bhagavan is here.

Towards the end of his bodily manifestation, he said, "They say that I am going, but where can I go? I am here."

Once when someone wrote a booklet criticising Sri Ramanasramam, Sri Bhagavan remarked that the author had done a great service to the cause of Truth. When asked for an explanation, he said that this book would keep away the insincere and superficial people and only the sincere Truth-seekers would continue to come. In the same way the Maharshi himself has done a great service to the cause of Truth by withdrawing himself from the physical plane. He has made himself unavailable to the worldly eye, while to the seeker with spiritual sight his living presence is very much here.

Om Namo Bhagavathe Sri Ramanaya!

૱ ૹ

# How I Came to Bhagavan

## Muhammad Abdulla

I WAS BROUGHT UP in rather religious surroundings and grew up a religious man. Later when I went to college and abroad my outlook changed. I became an agnostic if not a downright atheist. This condition lasted till my late thirties. All this time, off and on, I tried to regain my faith but to no avail. Somehow the idea of an anthropomorphic God did not appeal to me. I could not see any reason why God created the world. If He wanted to prove Himself to Himself, it seemed rather a poor reason. To create the world as a puppet show and enjoy it as a spectator also seemed ungodly and rather cruel.

Many questions troubled me. What is God? What is life? What is it all about? Scriptures did not satisfy me for they demanded faith to begin with, which I did not have. I studied psychology but there was nothing beyond the unconscious mind. I turned to dialectical materialism but then again I found that its adherents were at loggerheads on trivialities. Turning to existentialism, I found it too morbid and depressing. Finally I turned to metaphysics and mysticism and that is where luck favoured me.

While I was searching for a clue to my problem, by chance I got hold of a book from the library shelf. It was an old edition of *Day by Day with Bhagavan*. I was not particularly interested when I started reading it, but as I progressed my indifference gave way to astonishment. Well, here at last there was someone who was reaching me. I read on with great enthusiasm and finished the book with a thirst for more. I placed an order to the Ashram Book Depot for all the books about Bhagavan. I had never waited more eagerly for anything than the book parcel. When it came I studied everything from cover to cover drinking deep from this source of true wisdom.

For a couple of months, I was immersed heart and soul in the teachings of Bhagavan. Here at last, all my questions were answered, all my doubts cleared. When I had imbibed his teaching, I planned a visit to the Ashram.

Now I must say a word or two about the visits to the Ashram. There is something in coming to and going from this place. Some mysterious force takes charge of you the moment you decide to go there. I met by chance an old devotee, Prof. K. Swaminathan, who is in charge of Ramana Kendra in New Delhi. He encouraged me to make the visit. I left New Delhi and arrived at the Ashram two days later. It was 2.30 p.m. I sat in the meditation hall facing Bhagavan's picture. He seemed so much alive. Such a kind and benevolent smile! I could not move my eyes away from him. I had no idea of the time when suddenly the dinner gong was sounded at 7.30 p.m.

I lived in the Ashram for a month, and meditated morning and evening. I found to my surprise that the problems which seemed monumental gradually receded to the background. The past became shadowy. Yesterday's desires made no sense and made me laugh. Apprehension for the future dwindled to nothing. I felt happy.

A month was quickly over and I travelled back with a heavy heart. I had only one prayer when I took leave of Bhagavan. I wanted to come again. I also prayed to Bhagavan to help me maintain the peace I had found for a long time. Both my prayers were answered. I came again and again. Bhagavan never forsook me in my hours of trials. I never let go of Bhagavan nor does he let go of me!

CB ⁊

# RAMANA'S UNIVERSAL PHILOSOPHY

## Dr. M. Hafiz Syed

### I

## Ramana Maharshi's Spiritual Philosophy of Life

IT IS ONLY the sage who has realised the Truth Eternal that keeps the flame of spiritual wisdom alive. He is the perennial source of inspiration to the earnest aspirant on the path of spiritual development. Without him the world would not have had the light of the spirit to dispel the darkness of material existence.

Of such wisdom is sage Sri Ramana, who embodies in himself the Truth that is beyond time and space, who stands supreme in the realm of spiritual attainment and who is the true benefactor of the whole of the human race. In him we see that glorious realization which at once, includes and transcends all religions through the revelation that the only true religion is the religion of the heart. His teachings give the clearest expression to that one, inexpressible, universal, spiritual experience, seeking which, every earnest aspirant treads the path of inward spiritual development. To such an aspirant the Maharishi's teachings are a revelation of that Truth Eternal which ever resides as one and is identical with himself.

The nature of the world — Reality — whatever it be — is no hurdle to one who follows the path pointed out by the Maharshi. His insistence is not so much on deciding the unreality of the world as on discovering the Self. In one of the books published some years ago by the Ashram, the Maharshi brings out his point of view in a striking manner in reply to a question as to whether the objectivity of the world is not an indisputable fact of sense perception and whether this objectivity is not itself proof positive of the world's reality. Here is the Maharshi's answer: "The world, which you say is real is really mocking you for seeking to prove its reality, while of your own Reality you are ignorant." Even if we are of the world, the Maharshi wants us to see things in their proper perspective. Discussions about the Reality or otherwise of the world, should be of secondary importance to the earnest seeker whose one aim should be to seek the Self, the 'I' of which he can have the least doubt and the quest whereof, can alone lead him to the one that alone is real.

That Reality requires no proof, for it is Self-evident. It requires no proof, for it is Self-existing (*Svata-siddha*). It requires no scholarly exposition, for it is Self-luminous (*Svaprakasa*). What is required is not the proof or refutation of anything, but the poise in and the realization of the ever-existent, unchanging Self or the *Atman*.

It would be interesting to note in this connection what the Maharshi says regarding the true nature of sleep, for this will give us an idea as to what the state of pure consciousness would be in relation to life as we know it. One is not really enveloped in ignorance, says the Maharshi, when one is actually asleep. Sleep is not a state of non- existence nor mere blankness as we suppose it to be. It is a pure state. And what we call the waking consciousness does not necessarily contribute to true knowledge.

It is really a state of ignorance, because as a rule we are forgetful or unaware of our real nature. The Maharshi uses a striking paradox in order to impress on us the all-comprehensive nature of pure consciousness. He says, "There is full awareness in sleep and total ignorance in the waking state," and adds, "The Self is beyond both knowledge and ignorance." To put it briefly, sleep, dream and waking are only different modes of our higher consciousness.

ETERNAL AWARENESS: What then is realization? What is the relation between our life experience of ignorant existence and the state of realization which is all-embracing? The Maharshi's exposition on this point is most illuminating. "Realization", he declares, "is here and now. It is nothing to be gained afresh. The Self is not 'reached', you are the Self."

Most of us are prone to think we have not yet realized the Self, that we are *ajnanis,* but the Maharshi reminds us that this is merely our own thought about ourselves and that is the real obstacle in the way. It is not some objectified Self that is declared to be eternal. Our awareness of the Self is itself eternal. They are one and identical. In the words of the Maharshi there has never been a time when we are not aware of That, the Self. It is the never-ending, timeless state and it is in It that we live, move and have our being.

CLEAREST DEFINITION: Elucidating further the same point Maharshi says that the happiness the mind feels when agreeable things are presented to it is nothing but the happiness inherent to the Self. On these occasions it is verily into the Self that one dives. But the association of ideas is responsible for foisting the inherent bliss in us on things extraneous, because the plugging into the Self was unconsciously done. If you do so consciously, with the conviction that comes from experience that you are identical with that happiness which is verily the Self, the only Reality, you call it realization. That is the most realistic definition of Self-realization, and shorn of all mystery it is the clearest one you can have on the subject.

A SHACKLE: Answering the question from the particular point of view of the individual who has to do some specific work, the Maharshi reiterates in his own words what Sri Krishna taught five thousand years ago. "Work performed with attachment is a shackle, whereas work done with detachment does not affect the doer who may be said to be in solitude, even while he is free from attachment and has no desire."

Just as renunciation is not retirement into the forest, solitude is not seclusion from life. The Maharshi considers that solitude is related more to the inner working of the mind of man than in keeping away from the active life of the outer world. Solitude is of the mind, not of the body. It is the attitude of supreme serenity with which one views the flow of events in life and does not signify from the highest point of view living in seclusion and retirement.

One of the finest definitions of renunciation ever given is vouchsafed to us by the Maharshi, who says, "The Self alone is permanent. Renunciation is the non-identification of the Self with the not-Self. When the ignorance which identifies the Self with the not-Self is removed, the latter ceases to exist and that is true renunciation."

This definition, so simple yet so profound, is at once concise and comprehensive.

One enquirer was puzzled as to what would be the effect of his daily actions, right or wrong, in afterlife. The ideal *Vedantin* that the Maharshi is, his answer is pregnant with meaning, revealing to us an insight into the philosophy of life as taught by the ancient *rishis*. "The Self of man has no beginning and no end. It is never born and It never dies." If this truth is accepted, no question of birth and death can arise. What is subject to birth and death is the earthly vesture of man, whose essential being is deathless.

WHAT IS MIND? To the aspirant on the path of Self-realization, there is no question so puzzling and so vital as that of mind control. Many are the methods and remedies suggested and most of them have been practised with varying degrees of success, but Maharshi's solution to this age-long problem is all his own and sheds new light on this apparently hopeless problem. The Maharshi says that, as a matter of fact, there is no mind to control, if the Self is realized. The Self shines when the mind vanishes. In the realized man the mind may be active or inactive, but the Self alone exists. For the mind, body and the world are not separate from the Self. They cannot remain apart from the Self. Can they be other than the Self? When one is aware of the Self and has fully established oneself in it, one has no reason to worry about these shadows which cannot in the least affect the serenity of the immutable Self.

In order to have a clear grasp of the Maharshi's unique teachings on this point, the question has to be considered in a little more detail. According to him the problem of mind control ceases to be a problem when the mind seeks its source within.

What is mind? Does it exist apart from the thoughts that come and go? What is the 'I' with which the mind identifies itself? What is the one basis of the entire thought activity? It is the endeavour, made here and now, to gather in and converge the mind at its source, to attune it to the Self which is the support of all thought activity. This is the most natural, direct and immediately effective method of controlling the mind. Every other conceivable practice has this fundamental defect, namely it tries to control the mind by sustaining it. These other methods of practice retain the veil of the mind and can therefore never reveal the Self. When one dives within, seeking the source of thought and has a glimpse of the Self, one knows the true nature of the mind as nothing but an unreal manifestation of the one Reality, the Self.

NO SUCH THING: The two essential aspects of this question of mind control, which the Maharshi seeks to impress on the earnest aspirant are (1) that from the true and ultimate point of view of the one Reality — the Self — there is no such thing as the mind, and (2) that the endeavour to control the mind on the contrary assumption that there is really something called the mind to be controlled, is bound to prove futile. Because the mind, considered as real, will never allow itself to be controlled, just as the thief will never allow himself to be caught by turning himself into a policeman. Under the pretentious garb of a policeman, he would elude his own arrest all the more effectively. Even so, if we give the mind the garb of reality we would never be able to control it. The Maharshi, therefore, expects us to disregard all limitations, which pertain only to the mind, and plunge headlong into a dauntless search for the real Self in us. When our attention is fully riveted to the Self as the source of thought, the mind is subdued and controlled quite naturally and without any effort.

This in short, is the direct and right way to what is called peace of mind. Maharshi's method of approach to the control

of mind deserves fullest consideration and sincere efforts if we
have failed in trying other methods of mind control.

# II

# Testimony of Islam to Bhagavan's Life and Teachings

THE GREATNESS OF Ramana Maharshi's unique life and
teachings consists in the fact that he was unacquainted with the
scriptures of the world and yet after his Self-realization the
knowledge of Infinity was open to him. To quote a line from
Patanjali's *Yoga Sutra*, "When an unlettered person's mind is made
one-pointed, the inner and outer knowledge is revealed to him.
He comes in direct contact with the supreme Source of his Being."

The devotees of Ramana are acquainted with his simple
and uneventful life. He lived a plain life to the end. He was
without any pose or pretensions. Not only that he was a great
teacher and lived in a high plane of his own but he was utterly
human in every day life. He had love and sympathy for every
living creature as a true Brahmin should have. He mended his
own stick, took part in the cutting of vegetables and cooking
some food now and then. His sense of unity and equality of
mankind was so great that he never accepted anything prepared
for himself but had it distributed equally to all persons present
in his hall. Men of every race, caste, creed, sex, high and low,
rich and poor, visited him and to him all were alike. He never
showed any preference to men of position or looked down upon
a pariah or a *panchama*. To him all were accessible.

So was the Prophet of Islam. He believed in the brotherhood of man and treated all men alike. He used to say to his followers, *Ana mislakum*, that is "I am one like you". To him Jew or gentile, Muslim or non- Muslim were alike. Whenever a non-Muslim visited him when he was sitting in his mosque engaged in prayer he would at once rise up from his seat, spread his own cloak and seat him respectfully. He mended his own shoes and patched up his own worn-out garment. Nothing was left in his household for the morrow. All that he received during the course of a day was distributed to the needy and the poor. He often said *Al faqr fakhri*, that is to say, 'poverty is my pride'. He took keen interest in the welfare of human beings and used to retire to a cave for spiritual meditation. Thus we see there is a close similarity between his life and that of our beloved Maharshi.

We all know how Maharshi repeatedly enjoined us to surrender completely to God's will and be at peace with all, sink and bury our differences. In fact once he said, "Burn them and turn to the abode of peace, your own heart." Islam is derived from the root Salama which means peace, tranquillity and finally surrender of oneself to the Divine. 'The word Islam', says Deutch, a German writer, 'implies absolute submission to God's will'. Hazrat Ali, the fourth Caliph, the son-in-law of the Prophet said that "No one can have any conception of God unless he knows his own Self." Thus confirming Bhagavan's repeated teachings in all his well known books.

One mystic poet says, "What I have done with myself, no one has ever done it for himself. Within my own house (body) I have lost the owner of my house (that is my own self)". Does it not bear testimony to Bhagavan's inspiring words?

Further it is said in the Quran, "We are of God and to Him shall we return"(*Quran*, Chapter II, verse 156). This clearly indicates whence we came and whither we are going. Man's inherent divinity is expressed in these unequivocal words of the *Quran*. "God breathed His own breath in the nostril of man. Man was created after the face of God."

In the Ghaznavids and Early Saljuq's period there was a great philosopher-poet *Nasir-e-Khusrau,* who was acknowledged as a mystic of a great order. In his poem *Raushani nama* on Self-knowledge he writes, bearing full testimony to Bhagavan's well-known teachings:

Know yourself; for if you know yourself
You will also know the difference between good and evil.
First become intimate with your own inner being,
Then become the commander of the whole company.
When you know yourself, you know everything;
When you know that, you have escaped from all evil.
You don't know your own worth, because you are like this;
You see God Himself, if you see yourself.
The nine spheres and seven stars are your slaves,
Yet you are your body's servant: that's a pity!
Don't be fettered to bestial pleasures
If you are a seeker of that supreme blessedness.
Be a real man and abandon sleep and fasting;
Pilgrim-like, make a journey into yourself.
What are sleep and fasting? The business of brute beasts;
It is by knowledge that your soul subsists.
Be wakeful for once: how long have you been sleeping?
Look at yourself: you're something wonderful enough.
Reflect now; regard from where you've come
And why you are now in this prison.
Break the cage; depart to your own celestial station;
Be an idol-breaker like Abraham, Azar's son.

You were created after this fashion for a purpose;
It will be a shame, if you neglect that purpose.
It is a shame for an angel to take orders from a devil;
It is a shame for a king to be servant to a doorkeeper.
Why must Jesus be blind?
It is wrong for *Karun* to be one-eyed.
You have snakes coiled over your treasure:
Kill those snakes, and be free of pain.
But if you feed them, you will become fearful,
You'll have nothing of that boundless treasure.
There's a treasure in your house, yet you're a beggar;
You have a salve in your hand, yet your heart is wounded.
You are asleep; how will you reach journey's end?
You weave charms, and are heedless of the treasure. Quick,
break the charm and take the treasure:
Take a little pain, and rid yourself of pain.

Jalaluddin Rumi, prince of mystics, quoted by R.A. Nicholson in his *Rumi, Poet and Mystic,* says:

Jalalu'l-Din was asked, "Is there any way to God nearer than the ritual prayer?" "No," he replied, "but prayer does not consist in forms alone. Formal prayer has a beginning and an end, like all forms and bodies and everything that partakes of speech and sound; but the soul is unconditioned and infinite: it has neither beginning nor end. The prophets have shown the true nature of prayer. . . . Prayer is the drowning and unconsciousness of the soul, so that all these forms remain without. At that time there is no room even for Gabriel, who is pure spirit. One may say that the man who prays in this fashion is exempt from all religious obligations, since he is deprived of his reason. Absorption in the Divine Unity is the soul of prayer."

"When a fly is plunged in honey, all the members of its body are reduced to the same condition, and it does not move. Similarly the term *istighraq* (absorption in God) is applied to one who has no conscious existence or initiative or movement. Any action that proceeds from him is not his own. If he is still struggling in the water, or if he cries out, 'Oh, I am drowning', he is not said to be in the state of absorption. This is what is signified by the words *Ana'l-Haqq*, 'I am God'. People imagine that it is a presumptuous claim, whereas it is really a presumptuous claim to say *'Ana'l-'abd,'* 'I am the slave of God' and *'Ana'l-Haqq,'* 'I am God', is an expression of great humility. The man who says,*'Ana'l-abd'* 'I am the slave of God,' affirms two existences, his own and God's, but he that says *'Ana'l-Haqq'* 'I am God' has made himself non-existent and has given himself up and says, 'I am God,' i.e.'I am naught, He is all: there is no being but God's.' This is the extreme of humility and self-abasement."

These two quotations bear fullest and clearest testimony to Bhagavan's teachings as embodied in his books *Self Enquiry* and *Who am I?* and others.

ॐ ॐ

# BHAGAVAN SRI RAMANA, THE LIGHT DIVINE

## Dr. T.M.P. Mahadevan

*(Excerpts from a speech delivered on a* Jayanti *day)*

IT IS DIFFICULT to speak on *Advaita*. It is more difficult to speak about Bhagavan. I am not going to speak as an intellectual, nor as a professor of philosophy, I am going to speak to you as one would to his brothers and sisters. I think I will succeed in expressing at least a little of what I feel about Bhagavan only when you forget my personality totally. It is only when the speaker's individuality completely recedes into the background that the *Advaita* can be understood at all; and Bhagavan Ramana, as I am fond of saying, is pre-eminently an *Advaita avatara*.

Today is the most blessed day for us, who by a stroke of good fortune, have come under the protective wings of our Bhagavan. The *ardra* day has been an auspicious day in the Hindu calendar. But it has been made more auspicious because Bhagavan chose to be born on that day, and this year his birthday has come on the eve of another holy day, *Makarasankranti*. We will be able to appreciate the greatness and grandeur of the life and teachings of Bhagavan if we ponder for a moment over the significance of these two great festivals—*Ardra* and *Makarasankranti*. *Ardra* marks the victory of Lord Siva over the demon Andhaka. The very name 'Andhaka' means the 'dark' and the 'blind', and 'Andhaka' is an allegory for *ajnana, avidya,* ignorance or *maya.* It was on the *Ardra* day that the Lord vanquished Andhaka in order that the world may be saved, in order that humanity may see the face of goodness. The myth of the conquest of Andhaka signifies the victory of the forces of light over those of darkness, of *vidya* over *avidya,* of the supreme good over all that is evil.

After killing the demon Andhaka the Lord danced his cosmic dance, the expression of supreme joy, which alone sustains the Universe. It is in commemoration of this great event that the image of Nataraja is taken out of the temples in procession on the *Ardra* day. In the year 1879, on this auspicious day the Nataraja image of the temple at Tiruchuli was being taken into the temple at the conclusion of the procession. It was at this moment that Bhagavan Ramana was born. So, it is significant that our Lord chose the auspicious day of *Ardra* for making His advent into this world.

*Makarasankranti,* again, marks the dawn of the day of the gods — the beginning of *Uttarayana.* Students of the *Mahabharata* will remember that the great Bhishma lay on a bed of arrows awaiting the dawn of *Uttarayana.* Today the gods are awake. They have begun to have another bright day. The month proceeding *Makarasankranti* is also a holy month for us Hindus. The month of *Mirgasirsha* is to the gods what the *Brahmamuhurtam* is to humans. Therefore we prepare ourselves during this month for the dawn of the divine day by rising early in the morning and singing the praise of the Lord. In the south, especially in the Tamil area, even today we find groups of devotees rising early in the morning and singing the praise of God in the villages and towns, singing and awakening those who slumber and who will not otherwise hear the call of the divine.

The drama of bridal mysticism as portrayed in the *Tiruppavai* of Andal and the *Tiruvembavai* of Manikavachakar is the great drama of the communion of the soul with God. And it is this consummation that is sought to be achieved by observing the *vrata* (penanace) in the month of Mirgasirsha. This year after that preparatory penance we have today entered the path of light, the path of divine light. It is supremely significant that we should be thinking of Bhagavan 'the light divine'. Bhagavan Ramana is the supreme and eternal light, which alone can save us from degradation and spiritual death. I am reminded of a *mantra* of the *Isavasya Upanishad* which describes in graphic terms the lot of those who are killers of the soul.

Those who are slayers of the Self go to demoniac worlds of blinding darkness enveloped in *ajnana*. If we do not want to share the fate of the soul-killers, we must turn our eyes away from those regions of blinding darkness and take to the straight path of spiritual light emblazoned before us by Bhagavan Sri Ramana. So on this auspicious occasion may we meditate on Bhagavan as the light divine.

The symbol of light as representing spiritual illumination is as universal as religion is. In mysticism and in spirituality there is no better symbol of the spirit than light. In Christianity the symbol of light is employed to denote the heavenly Father and the heavenly Son equally. One of the pictures that impressed me when I was young and continues to fascinate me is that of Jesus Christ holding a lighted lantern in one hand and knocking at the door of a house with the other, bearing the inscription, "Behold the light of the world."

The Buddha has been described as the light of Asia. Zoroastrianism thinks of God as the luminous Fire. The Konarak Temple, which I visited recently, is a great monument of the

devotion of the Hindu for the symbol of the sun. One finds
there various aspects of the solar principle expressed in beautiful
sculpture. Sun-worship is not foreign to India. The sun cult
*(Saura-mata)* is one of the oldest forms of Hinduism. In the
*mantras* of *Rig Veda* we have different aspects of the solar
principle adored and we come across names of various solar
deities. The Gayatri *mantra* signifies a grand mode of meditating
on the principle that is behind the sun. The adored principle is
the worshipful splendour of the solar deity.

The supreme splendour of the solar deity we invoke and
meditate on every day so that our intellects may be purified
thereby. To characterise the *Vedic* deities as the personification
of natural phenomena is not to understand what the ancient
seers and saints saw in their inward turned vision. It was not the
physical phenomena that they worshipped, but the spiritual
principle behind nature. They also discovered that the same
principle pervades everything, objective as well as subjective.
Between the external and the internal there is correspondence
in principle. For instance, all *Upanishadic* text identifies the god
that is in the sun with the principle that is in the right eye.
What is in the macrocosm is identical with what is in the
microcosm. We find this truth expressed exquisitely in the form
of a prayer in the *Isavasya Upanishad.*

No poet of mean order, no worshipper of the natural
phenomena could have composed this grand verse. The spiritual
principle behind the solar phenomena is recognised here, and it
is this spiritual principle that is prayed to in this verse. Consider
the grand closing of this *mantra*, where there is a *Mahavakya*
uttered: *yosavasan purusah soham asmi.* The principle that is yonder,
miles and miles away, in the sun is the same principle that is
within me. I am He. Thus in Hinduism we find the true

significance of sun-worship expressed. Then we are told that the consummation of such worship is the realisation of non-duality, the realisation of *abedha,* non-difference. The symbol of light is not an empty symbol. It is sublime in its significance. Sri Ramana represents the supreme light of spirituality which knows no distinction and which knows no difference.

The birth of Bhagavan is itself a manifestation of that spiritual illumination. In order to lift us to the spiritual heights, in order to attract us to the supreme goal, he incarnated himself as a human being, and lived and moved in our midst. We know that Bhagavan as a student did not belong to the extraordinary type. He was not brilliant, nor even studious. But how this ordinary lad received illumination all of a sudden cannot be explained. How this could happen passes our understanding. The little candle of our intellect cannot illumine the self-effulgent sun. To attempt to understand the secret of Bhagavan's life is bound to end in failure. All that we can do is to meditate on him as the light eternal, the light supreme.

Look at another marvel. Some relative of his who came to his uncle's house in Madurai one day said that he was coming from Arunachala. But what Arurnachala was, what it meant, our Bhagavan did not know. Yet this word acted like a magic spell and drew him out of his uncle's house to that Hill which is no ordinary Hill, but which is the Hill of spiritual light. The Hill which represents spiritual light drew unto itself the light that was born in Tiruchuli. This light travelled to 'The Hill of the Holy Beacon', and what appeared as two lights were recognised to be one.

The story about Tiruvannamalai (Arunachala) is itself significant, as are the festivals connected with Bhagavan's birth. The Creator Brahma and the Protector Vishnu are said to have

quarrelled between themselves as to who was superior. In order
to teach them a lesson Lord Siva appeared as a column of light
without top or bottom. Brahma and Vishnu could not discover
the limits of the light-column. It is this limitless light that
Arunachala represents. Bhagavan found in Arunachala the light
supreme, which he himself is.

Bhagavan did not leave the precincts of Arunachala after
his arrival there. Why should he go anywhere? When the world
was ready to go to him, why should he go to the world? The
world should go to the guru. There is no use of the guru going
to the world. Because if he goes to the world he would only be
misunderstood. Even Sri Krishna had to confess that he was not
being understood by the people.

"Because I have taken birth as a human being people do
not understand me. On the contrary, they scold me, they abuse
me, they revile me."

The world knows only to revile things! Even Arjuna,
Krishna's own cousin and dear disciple, could not understand
the magnificence of the supreme Master. The Lord had to reveal
his cosmic form in order to drive sense into Arjuna's head. Arjuna
repents for his past behaviour and says, "Out of familiarity and
not knowing your greatness, I have called you, ' O Krishna, O
Yadava, O friend.' Please forgive me for whatever disrespect I
have shown towards you." Because of his easy accessibility Sri
Krishna was not understood by the world. The world seldom
understands the guru who goes to it.

It is only when the world has learned to go to the guru
that the world will feel inclined to listen to him. Sri Ramana
had no need of going to the world whilst he lived in Arunachala.
The world, even the western world went to him. Why did this
happen? Bhagavan was the light transcendent which cannot be

resisted. If you try to resist it today, by a greater force you will be attracted to it tomorrow. Light does not require darkness for making it acceptable. Only darkness does. You need not paint light because it is all luminous. Without advertisement, without any drum beating, without any concerted propaganda, the light that was at Arunachala spread far and wide, and it is on that light that we should meditate. We saw before our eyes the grand manifestation of that majestic light. We saw the grandeur of that spiritual light before us. If we could not see it, it was our fault, and not that of the light. In order that you may understand light, the light need not speak to us. It is only when there is darkness that you require the help of speech in order to identify the things around, but when there is light and when your eyes are all right you need not be told what is around you.

And so, for the most part, Bhagavan Ramana kept silent. Silence was his mode of communication. Today people all over the world are striving hard to find out new means of communication. But in spite of the many devices, communication becomes more and more difficult. Here, without any verbal communication for the most part, the blessed Lord, seated or reclining on his couch in the corner of the old hall in the Ashram, was communicating not only with those who sat before him, but with devotees who were even far away. Though most of us may not understand for the moment the language of silence, we are sure to understand it eventually. Our Bhagavan did not move out of Arunachala and seldom did he speak. Even his speech was of a quality that is far different from the speech that we are accustomed to. His speech was scarcely distinguishable from silence. Some of us had opportunities of watching the grand silent drama that was being enacted constantly in that auspicious hall. People came, strangers came with long lists of questions to test the Maharshi, but often it so happened that those who came with doubts forgot all about them. They forgot to question because there was no need to ask. What they had come for had already been fulfilled.

The most remarkable feature about Bhagavan's form was his eyes, extremely penetrating and profoundly fascinating. Once you had come within the range of those beaming eyes, there was no need for any other *sadhana*. Once those eyes had rested upon you there was no more fear or worry for you. The very first European to see our Master, Humphrys, who sent reports to a magazine in England, has made this statement: 'For half an hour I looked into the Maharshi's eyes, which never changed their expression of deep contemplation.' This was written as early as in 1911. Those of us who met the Master much later could testify that the brightness of those eyes did not diminish at all, not even on the last day of the his earthly existence.

Last summer in Honolulu some American professors of philosophy happened to look at the picture of the Master that appears as frontispiece in the book *Ramana Maharshi and His Philosophy of Existence*. Many of them wanted to have copies of this book even before reading what was written there, just because the face of the Master fascinated them, enraptured them. All of them, without exception remarked about the remarkable eyes. From those eyes, light shone forth from which no one could escape. Bhagavan out of compassion for us, who cannot understand the language of silence, did sometimes speak, but not for the sake of speaking as most of us do. He wrote not for the sake of writing, because he was no writer at all. He spoke and wrote because he wanted to save us.

There is a fine *sloka* in the *Aankaradigvijaya* where Vidyaranya offers obeisance to Dakshinamuthi and Sankara:

"Rising from his seat beneath the banyan tree, and breaking His silence, Dakshinamurti, out of compassion for humanity which is being burnt in the forest-fire of *samsara*, took form as Sankara who moved about constantly and spoke profusely. The silent Dakshinamurti became the speaking Sankara. The unmoving began to move."

Bhagavan Ramana struck a compromise between the silence and stasis of Dakshinmurti and the speech and movement of Sankara, because today we require the message of both *atchara* and *chara, mauna* and *vak.* Bhagavan Ramana spoke and wrote in order that we may understand him. The path of light that he has expounded in what he has written and spoken is the same path of light which has come from the ancient sages and seers of the *Upanishads.* The light of *jnana* is what we ought to strive for and gain. It is this which can save us. And this is the central message of Bhagavan, the light divine. What is this light? It is the light *of Atma vichara,* the light of Self-enquiry. This light can be gained by anyone, any human being, no matter what his beliefs are, or where he is born. The *Upanishads* set forth various modes of Self-enquiry. Only our Bhagavan has made Self-enquiry easy for us, and has simplified it so that all of us can adopt it and follow it and gain what it alone can give us. And also he has given us a technique by which we can register quick results. He rediscovered for us the heart that is on the right side of the chest. By fixing the attention on this heart, the spiritual heart, the path of enquiry, a discovery made in *Vedanta,* our Bhagavan has given to us out of compassion.

It will be interesting to note that the great *Upanishadic* sage Yagnavalkya in one of his teachings to King Janaka employs the significant phrase, '*hrdyantar-jyotih*', in describing the self-- the Atma, the light which is within the heart.

One day when the Sage walked into the king's court, the king put to him a question. It was: "What serves as the light for man?"

The Master began by saying that "the sun is light for man." "During daytime it is by the light of the sun that we work".

Then the king asked, 'When the sun has set, what is man's light?" "The moon", came the answer. "We do work with the help of the light of the moon; when the sun has set, the moon acts as the light for us."

"But what happens during the absence of moonlight?" asked the king. "What serves as the light then?" "Fire!" said the master. "You may light a fire, you may burn a lamp and work with the help of the light it gives."

"And when fire goes out, what has one to do? There is no sun, moon. or fire!"

"In such a situation speech can serve as the principle of illumination. For instance, when we go through a dark region where no light is there, we clap our hands or we speak in order to hearten those who may follow us", continued the master.

"When speech, sir, is also not there, what serves as light for man?"

The final reply of the Master came, "The Self. The Self, Self luminous light."

What happens to us when we dream? There is not the external sun, nor the moon, nor fire, nor even speech, and yet there is experience. The Self of the dream state is therefore called *taijasa* (made of light). In the absence of any light there is experience, there is luminosity. The Self is of the nature of consciousness. It is that which shines in the recesses of one's heart. This is the great teaching of *Vedanta* and Bhagavan. So long as we trust the light of the mind, we are sure to be misguided. It is only when we turn to the light of the heart that we shall be saved. The great danger that confronts the modern man is that he believes in the omnipotence of the light of the mind. He scans space. He wants to travel through it. He wants to know what is on the other side of the moon. He wants to colonise the planets and the stars if he can, all with the help of this light of the mind. He has not opened the door of his heart, and so he is threatened by what he has created by the light of his mind. What man has created now dominates him like a Frankenstein and threatens him with utter destruction.

What does Bhagavan teach us? He does not want us to shut out the light of the mind. "With the help of the mind, he says, "let us enter the region of the heart." When you turn to the light of the heart, you will know that the mind shines only by borrowed light. The original light is there. It is that resplendent light which is the supreme Self. It is this which is called *Hrdyantar-jyotih* (light within the heart).

Bhagavan found its location on the right side of the chest. It is not the physical heart which is on the left side, it is the spiritual heart. Not that it is there physically. The surgeon's knife cannot exhibit it. It is the spiritual heart which Bhagavan Ramana located on the right side of the chest, so that we may meditate on it and gain progress in the path of *jnana*. How should one enquire? Bhagavan has given us a wondrous method. It is the simple enquiry of 'Who am I?' Bhagavan Ramana held that the word *'Aham'*, is the most sacred of all *mantras*, more sacred even than the *Pranava* itself. It is more efficacious than all the *mantras*. This again is a true discovery of Bhagavan. It is true that the *Pranava* is the sound-symbol of Brahman. But what is easier to understand is *'Aham'* (I). You may deny everything else but you cannot deny the Self.

*Aham* is often meant to signify the non-Self. Even the 'I' thought is not the real 'I'. It is the pseudo 'I'. In order to overcome this, it has to be used in a judicious way. One must trace the 'I' thought to its source. When this is done, with constant and persistent inquiry, the distinction between the thinker and thought is found to vanish and then the Self which is pure experience will be realised. This path is the same as the *asparsa*-yoga taught by Gaudapada. It is the path that leads to non-duality, the path which takes us away from the non-Self. Ordinarily, man runs along the mental current, goes out through the sense-channels and gets lost in the external world. But one in a million, the hero, *dhira* as the *Upanishads* call him, has the strength to go against the current, swim in the reverse direction, and reach the source of the mental current. This is the path of *vichara* which is easy and yet difficult. Seemingly easy, even a child can pursue this course at the beginning, but he cannot gain its end if he chooses to remain childish all the time. It is true that anyone can take to it but he must pay the price for it. The price is dispassion. This does not mean that one must neglect one's duties. When *sadhakas* asked Bbagavan, "Is it necessary that one should leave one's house, change the colour of one's clothes and go to the forest," Bhagavan used to say, "No, it is wrong to think that you will become a new man by simply leaving home. If you go to the forest your home will haunt you, it will follow you. Can you leave your mind behind, your sense organs or your body? What binds you is not your family, or home, but your mind. How to renounce the mind? To renounce does not mean sitting in a place closing the eyes and thinking 'I have renounced.' That is not true renunciation. True renunciation is to become mindless. How is this to be accomplished? Through inquiry. Trace the mind to its source with the help of the mind itself. Catch the thief with the help of the thief. Through *Atma vichara*, we get to the end where there is no mind at all. If you cannot do this, if you do not have the strength to follow this method," says Bhagavan, "surrender yourself to God. Absolute self-surrender is *bhakti*." In Bhagavan's hymns on Arunachala we have a glorious philosophy of devotion. The quintessence of this philosophy is to negate yourself in the Lord and you will find fulfilment. Let God pervade your being then you will be saved. Even this is difficult for many of us. We worship God with commercial spirit. We seek earthly benefits from Him.

A *sanyasin* went to the palace of a king in the hope of receiving alms. The king was engaged at the time in worshipping his chosen deity. His prayer was, "Give me this, give me that." The *sanyasin* was listening to this prayer; and after a while he rose to leave the palace. The king came out and asked him why he was leaving. The *sanyasin* said, "I came to beg but I now find that you are a greater beggar. How can I beg of you when you yourself beg for this and that in your private shrine?"

We go to God for gaining selfish ends. There are *phalasrutis* which say 'If you recite this prayer, you will get your desires fulfilled'. I am not condemning or criticising this, but I want you to understand the significance of the *phalasrutis*. When a *phalasruti* says, 'If you recite the *Vishnu-sahasra nama* your desires will be fulfilled', this is only with a view to making people turn God-ward and recite His name. But when once you have tasted the sweetness of the name you will not care for the earthly benefits.

When you go to God therefore, what you should do is to surrender yourself to Him completely. But this too is difficult. And so what should one do? We must resign ourselves into the hands of the guru, Bhagavan Ramana. This is the purpose of a celebration like this. If we can surrender ourselves, especially those of us who have seen him and have heard him speak, we shall be saved. Even others can follow this course because he has not gone away from us. It is not that he is no longer with us. Even now he guides those who go to him. The reality which is the Self shines within those who go to him. Even today he will guide us provided that we seek his guidance.

Bhagavan has declared in two short lines the entire teaching of *Vedanta*:

> *Ekam aksharam hrdi nirantaram,*
> *bhasate svayam likhyate katham.*

The Reality which is the Self shines within the heart always. How can one write about it?

If we can realise within the heart the supreme Spirit, if we can feel its presence, if we allow ourselves to be illumined by it, we shall have no fear at all. At the commencement of the fourth chapter of the *Mandukya-kharika* Gaudapada offers obeisance to Lord Narayana, the first guru. We may offer the same obeisance to our Bhagavan. *Jnana* is like *akasa*, the supreme Self which is to be known through *jnana* is also like ether. The various objects we see in the world as well as the souls are like ether. Therefore, who is to know which? What is to be known by what? The supreme realization is that there is no plurality. True knowledge is distinctionless. That knowledge is the Self, the Light Divine. That knowledge is Bhagavan Ramana.

May we offer our obeisance to this supreme Lord who came to save the world and who still abides and will ever abide with us in order to make us perfect!

May we, on this auspicious occasion, renew our faith in our Bhagavan and pay homage to Him so that not only we, but the entire world may be saved!

# SRI RAMANA:
# A PURE CHANNEL FOR
# A HIGHER POWER

## Paul Brunton

FORTY YEARS* have passed since I walked into his abode and saw the Maharshi half-reclining, half-sitting on a tiger-skin covered couch. After such a long period most memories of the past become somewhat faded, if they do not lose their existence altogether. But I can truthfully declare that, in his case, nothing of the kind has happened. On the contrary, his face, expression, figure and surroundings are as vivid now as they were then. What is even more important to me is that - at least during my daily periods of meditation - the feeling of his radiant presence is as actual and as immediate today as it was on that first day.

So powerful an impression could not have been made, nor continued through the numerous vicissitudes of an incarnation which has taken me around the world, if the Maharshi had been an ordinary yogi - much less an ordinary man. I have met dozens

* Written in 1971

of yogis, in their Eastern and Western varieties, and many exceptional persons. Whatever status is assigned to him by his followers, or whatever indifference is shown to him by others, my own position is independent and unbiassed. It is based upon our private talks in those early days when such things were still possible, before fame brought crowds; upon observations of, and conversations with, those who were around him; upon his historical record; and finally upon my own personal experiences, whatever they are worth.

Upon all this evidence one fact is incontrovertibly clear — that he was a pure channel for a Higher Power.

This capacity of his to put his own self-consciousness aside and to let himself be suffused by this Power, is not to be confounded with what is commonly called in the West, spiritualistic mediumship. For no spirit of a departed person ever spoke through him: on the contrary, the silence which fell upon us at such times was both extraordinary and exquisite. No physical phenomena of an occult kind was ever witnessed then; nothing at all happened outwardly. But those who were not steeped too far in materialism to recognise what was happening within him and within themselves at the time, or those who were not congealed too stiffly in suspicion or criticism to be passive and sensitive intuitively, felt a distinct and strange change in the mental atmosphere. It was uplifting and inspiring; for the time being it pushed them out of their little selves, even if only partially.

This change came every day, and mostly during the evening periods when the Maharshi fell into a deep contemplation. No one dared to speak then and all conversations were brought to an end. A grave sacredness permeated the entire scene and evoked homage, reverence, even awe. But before the sun's departure brought about this remarkable transformation, and for most of the day, the Maharshi behaved, ate and spoke like a perfectly normal human being.

That there was some kind of a participation in a worldless divine play during those evenings - each to the extent of his own response - was the feeling with which some of us arose when it all ended. That the Maharshi was the principal actor was true enough on the visible plane. But there was something more .

In his own teachings Sri Ramana Maharshi often quoted, whether in association or confirmation, the writings of the first Acharya Shankara, who lived more than a thousand years ago. He considered them unquestionably authoritative. He even translated some of them from one Indian language to another.

In the temple of Chingleput I interviewed His Holiness the Shankaracharya of Kamakoti Peetam, a linear successor of the first Guru. When the meeting was concluded but before I left, I took the chance to ask a personal question. A disciple of the Maharshi had come to me and wanted to take me to his Guru. None of those I asked could tell me anything about him, nor had even heard of him. I was undecided whether to make the journey or not.

His Holiness immediately urged me to go, and promised satisfaction. He is still alive and still active in the religious world of Southern India.

Sometimes, as I looked at the figure of Ramana Maharshi on the couch, I wondered if he would ever come to England. If so, how would he be dressed, how would he behave in those teeming London streets, how would he eat, live and work? But he was uninterested in travelling and so he never came, not in the physical body: what did come was his spirit and mind, which have awakened sufficient interest among the English.

Again and again he gave us this teaching, that the real
Maharshi was not the body which people saw; it was the inner
being. Those who never made the journey to India during his
life time may take comfort in this thought that it is possible to
invoke his presence wherever they are, and to feel its reality in
the heart.

ॐ

# PART III

# ON
# MISCELLANEOUS
# TOPICS

# THE ETERNAL NOW

## Major A.W. Chadwick (Sadhu Arunachala)

IN MANY OFFICES one finds the encouraging notice, 'Do it Now!' Although this is undoubtedly good advice, it is hardly to my present point, as I contend that we can never do it any "when" else. It always is NOW and the sooner we realize this the quicker will problems and worries disappear. Sri Bhagavan has the following verse on the subject of time in his *Forty Verses* (verse XV) :

> The future and the past are only seen
> With reference to the present. They in turn
> Are present too. The present's only true.
> As well to search for future and for past
> Outside the eternal present of the Self,
> As think to count without unit One,
> Which sums up the subject succinctly.

I have long been intrigued by this question of time. Some few years ago I saw Anand Coomaraswamy's book *Time and Eternity*, but unfortunately neglected to take notes of the many apposite quotations contained therein on the subject. The few that do follow I have noted myself, at various times in my varied reading.

St. Augustine, that pillar of Christianity, was himself much puzzled by this question and prayed to God for enlightenment. In his book *'Confessions'* , he has the following: 'Neither the past nor the future, but only the present really is; the present is only a moment and time can only be measured while it is passing. Nevertheless, there really is time past and future'. We seem here to be led into contradictions. The only way we can avoid this is to say that the past and future can only be thought of as present. Past must be identified with memory, and future with expectation, memory and expectation both being present fact.

This, after all, is much the same as Bhagavan's verse although St. Augustine is not quite certain of himself and hesitates to speak outright.

One of the last of the great western philosophers, Kant, found in time, one of the basic premises of his whole philosophy. He declared that "time is not an empirical concept derived from any experience"..... "only on the presupposition of time can we represent to ourselves a number of things as existing at one and the same time or at different times" . . . ...

"Time is a necessary representation that underlies all intuition. We cannot in respect of appearances in general remove time itself, though we can quite well think time as devoid of appearances. Time is therefore given *a priority*". In other words we cannot think outside time. Time is one of the modes of our minds as thinking machines. Bhagavan also asks in *Forty Verses* (verse XVI): "Do time and space exist apart from us?" Implying thereby, the contrary.

In our objectification of the world, we create it in terms of time and space, thus only can we see it apart from ourselves. In the 'eternal now' it ceases entirely to exist. We find it hard to realize this as our minds are restless machines and refuse to give up activities which necessitate time for their functioning. We are always trying to become something else, other than what we are, or rather think we are at the moment — happy and virtuous, failing to see that all becoming must change, so that this happiness gained will change back into its opposite eventually, that is into unhappiness. It is only in 'being' or the 'now' that we can ever find rest. Plato also says that time and creation come into existence together, in fact all appearance is only in time. And Schopenhauer opines that matter is actual, (using actual in its original meaning), that is only in its functioning, which is in time, so does it exist at all?

My reading of the Hindu Scriptures is defective, though undoubtedly, they must say exactly the same repeatedly. I find I am unable to quote from them as I should to substantiate my thesis, but I know one quotation from the *Vishnu Purana,* which finds its place here. Parasuram says, "Time is only a form of Vishnu, for change is only possible for things which are imagined with reference to a substratum."

But the whole picture, all our waking experiences, is only one moment in eternity. We see only a part and through continuing time, a strip. It all depends on the angle from which we look at it, as to what we see. If we look repeatedly from the same angle we see the same isolated picture or strip. The picture never changes, it is only our point of view. The prophet is able to see a larger expanse of the picture than the layman. To merge entirely in the picture is to know eternity and from that view point there is no picture as we know it, and no time.

Boethus, the old Roman statesman awaiting his death in prison also said, "Eternity is the simultaneous and complete possession of Infinite Life." It would be hard to find it summed up better than this. For eternity is the 'now', it does not flow in time, there is no before or after in it, no birth and no death.

Heraclitus, the Greek famous for the aphorism: "Everything flows," said that fire was the cause of all. By this he did not mean the physical fire, but rather the energy of the modern scientists, though an energy that was not just material but rather spiritual. For him this central fire is eternal and never dies, "the world was, is ever, and ever shall be, an ever-living fire." Although fire itself is everlastingly changing, this change would, like phenomena, seem to be apparent, but essentially fire remains the same fire. Change in appearance is its nature, as 1:9 *Mandukyopanishad* has it: 'Others think that manifestation is for the purpose of God's fulfilment. While still others attribute it to mere diversion. But it is the very nature of the effulgent being, for what desire is possible for him whose desire is always fulfilled?'

Substitute fire for effulgent being, which is after all a legitimate substitution, for what is fire but effulgent? And do not both of these essentially agree?

In Bergson I find the following sentence: "Pure duration is the form which our conscious states assume when our ego lets itself live, when it refrains from separating its present state from its former states." This apparently goes beyond the tenets of *Advaita*, as he seems to be referring to the reincarnating ego in his reference to former states, nevertheless it is pregnant with meaning, for we are undoubtedly conscious when we rest in the now, although we do not individualise. Surely it is only then that we do really live!

For many of the philosophers, time was a problem, with the exception of those who considered it to be something real, although we are little interested at the moment in their conclusions as we are trying to picture the verity of the 'eternal now', in contrast to the unreality of time, which slips through our fingers like a running stream when the hand is plunged into the water to stay its course.

Leaving the realms of metaphysics let us glance at the hypotheses of some of the scientists. They have certainly been intrigued by the problem and well understood that it was not to be ignored. Especially since Einstein sprang on the world his theory of relativity. He himself says in one place that distance is between events and not things, which takes a matter-of-fact measurements out of the realm of every day life, where we thought they were safely enthroned and could be relied upon, into the province of time itself, where we had never thought that time had any reason to interfere.

It reminds us of Schopenhauer's 'matter is actual', though one doubts if he ever really intended to imply quite as much as this. He does say, "All being in time is also non-being, for time is only that by means of which opposite determinations, can belong to the same thing. Therefore every phenomenon, which is in time again is not. For what separates its beginning from its end is only time, which is essentially a flitting, inconstant and relative thing."

In astronomy time takes on its most intriguing aspect. We think that when we look through our telescopes into the measureless distances of the sky, we are looking at something present now. Most of what we see has either moved millions of miles away from where it appears to be or has even ceased to exist altogether. We are, in fact, looking at all sorts of things which are not there at all. And if this cannot be called *maya* then the term has no meaning. One of the furthest nebulae our present telescopes can reach is 150 million light years away, an unimaginable mathematical figure. What actually does this mean? It means that the astronomer now is looking at a 150 million year past event, which is happening for him in the present. At best he is only looking at a cosmic memory. The picture does not actually exist at all.

The whole pattern of the heavens, the position of the stars is an hallucination; they have one and all moved away from the positions in which we see them now, but not proportionately, so that the actual pattern is much the same. But some have shifted vast distances and others but little in comparison. We may photograph it, plot it on our tracing board, all to no purpose. It is all a myth. Our sight and even our machines are grossly deceived as we can never know what the picture really is. Even the apparent stationary position of the stars is deceptive. They are one and all rushing about at incredible speeds. Time is playing a game with us.

Eddington pointed out that if the Universe is spherical whatever direction we may look, provided there is no obstruction, we would be able to see the back of our own heads. Well not exactly! Because time has taken over 6,000 million years to go round and our heads were not there then, we ought to be able to see what stood in that particular place then. Now let us suppose there are no obstructions and we do see some object which existed in that spot 6,000 million years ago, what actually does it signify? We see and yet we don't see. We really see an object that is not there at all. Our head is turned by such riddles and with the poet Omar Khayam, who was himself a great astronomer, we may truly say,

"Another and another cup to drown
The memory of this Impertinence."

Perhaps this same problem was too much for him also. We can hardly be surprised.

So it would seem as if science were gradually being forced to recognize that reality can alone be found in the 'eternal now', and that time deceives us every step we take. Each of us makes his own individual picture in terms of time and space, which spring up together with the uprising ego and with it, sinks back again. As Bhagavan says:

"The ego rising all else will arise.

On it subsiding, all will disappear."

(*Forty Verses on Reality,* verse 26)

Is it not also written in the book of Revelation X. 5. 6.? "And the angel which I saw stand upon the sea and the earth lifted up his hand to heaven and swore by him that liveth for ever and ever . . . . that there should be time no longer."

As a method of meditation trying to rest in the 'now' irrespective of time is interesting and seems to me a productive *sadhana*. When all is at rest and the flow of outward events is allowed to go on itsway unheeded, or taken up together into the whole, a peace passing all understanding rests on one and one draws very near to a full realization of the Reality. I am not speaking here of *nirvikalpa samadhi* when all outward cognizance has disappeared, but rather of a preliminary condition. As for the ultimate state it matters little whether we call it the Self, Eternal Now, or pure Being. These are all names only given in objective consciousness. In pure introspection they are found to be one and the same.

For the *advatin* who sees and knows the One alone, such discussion may seem unproductive and for some not even interesting, But for those who are not so established, there still remain doubts and especially on the question of mortality. They fear death. They look on it as extinction. And the dogmas and creeds of various faith give them no more than encouraging words, not assurance, but in the certainty of the Eternal Now, all such doubts should be dispelled. Here, there can be no fear of death, for how can we ever escape from the present that is now. It eternally is. And it is summed up by, I AM. Not I was or I may be at some future date, but eternally I AM.

Schopenhauer endorses this, "any form of life or reality is really only the *present*, neither the future nor the past. These are only in the conception . . . .    No man has ever lived in the past, and none will ever live in the future. The present alone is the form of all life, and is its sure possession which can never be taken from it. *The present* always *exists*."

But I begin to overstep the space allowed me. So I will end with one last quotation from Plato:

"Now all these portions of time, and *was* and *shall be*, are forms of time which have come to be, although we wrongly ascribe them to the eternal essence. For we say that it was and is and shall be, but in reality *is* alone belongs to it."

ᐸ᙮ᐳ

# THERE IS NOTHING, BE!

## Major A. W. Chadwick (Sadhu Arunachala)

THE PHILOSOPHY OF Sri Bhagavan, the greatest of sages, can be summed up in just three words "There is nothing." So simple and yet so supremely difficult. "There is nothing." All this world that you see, this mad rush of people after money and 'existence' is just a fabricless thought. "There is nothing." You, as a personality, as a petty entity striving for your own selfish ends, ever seeking so-called 'Self-Realisation', are nothing. You are like the shadow of a leaf cast by the moonlight, intangible, unsubstantial, and in fact non-existent. And, as the shadow is a purely negative phenomenon, is in fact nothing but a shutting out of light, so is the ego and everything else (because everything follows in the train of the ego and is actually a part of it) only a shutting out of the light of the Self.

Sri Bhagavan tells us just one other thing. He says: "Be. Just be your real Self, that's all." "Certainly, it sounds all right," you say, "but when one tries to do it, it does not seem so easy. Has he no method?"

Method! Well, what exactly do you mean by method? Sitting on the floor and concentrating on the navel? Or blowing the wind out of alternate nostrils? Or repeating some incantation one crore and eight times? No, he hasn't got any method. All these things are no doubt good in their way and help to prepare one, but Sri Bhagavan doesn't happen to teach them.

"Then what am I to do?"

You must just BE, he says. And to be you must know the 'I that is.' To know the 'I that is', just go on enquiring 'Who am I?' Don't take any notice of anything except the 'I', throw everything else away like refuse. And when you have at last found the 'I', BE. All talk, all empty words. 'There is nothing' and that's the end of it. No method, nothing to discard, nothing to find. Nothing at all is except the 'I'. Why worry about anything else? Just BE, now and always, as you were, as you are, and as you ever will be.

'There is nothing.' You may justly ask, "Who wants this purely negative state?"

To which I can only reply: "It is just a question of taste." Though, note you, I have never suggested that Sri Bhagavan ever says that the ultimate state after which, it is presumed, we are all striving is negative. On the contrary, when he says: "There is nothing", it is obvious that he is speaking about our present egoistic existence, which for us is everything. But this being where there is nothing must obviously be a state which is something. That state is Self-realisation. Not only is it something but it is EVERYTHING, and being everything then logically and philosophically it must be PERFECT.

"If we are already perfect and there is nothing else, what need is there for us to go to Bhagavan?" you ask.

And this reminds me of a story against myself.

An Australian journalist came to the Ashram, quite why he came is a mystery, I doubt if he would be able to tell himself. Anyhow he did come and in the course of his visit came to see me in my room. It was obvious from the first moment that I was a tremendous problem to him. Why a European should shut himself away in a place like this was beyond his comprehension. He asked many questions but none of my replies satisfied him. How could they? Especially as he had not the first idea of what the Ashram was, or what people were doing here. I didn't even write, then what on earth did I do? At length he could contain himself no longer and bluntly asked me what I was doing here. Now here was a problem to answer. If I had tried to tell him the truth he would never have understood, that I realized, so making the best of it I just said that here I found peace of mind. I knew it was an inadequate answer but hoped it would stave off further enquiries.

He looked at me seriously for a few minutes and then said pityingly: "Oh I see, I have never been troubled in that way myself!"

All I had succeeded in doing was in confirming him in the conviction that I was insane! And was there not, after all, some ground for his belief? Here have I been spending ('wasting', he would say) half a lifetime searching for something I already possess. I know that I possess it too, which makes matters appear worse.

'Just BE.' It sounds so easy. Well, Sri Bhagavan says it's the easiest thing there is. I really don't know. I suppose it all really depends on how much refuse there is inside. We're all different anyway and perhaps some of us were handicapped at the start. It's certain that the rubbish has to come out and the coming out process is full of surprises. All kinds of hidden vices and evil tendencies start to pop up their heads which one never suspected were there at all. But it's all for the good. Bhagavan says they have to come out. But let them come out, not take charge. Don't give way to them.

Those who expect Sri Bhagavan to hand them Self-realisation, as if it were some tangible thing, are surely sadly deluded. How can anybody give one what one has already got? All he can do is help one to remove the ignorance that hides it. It is like going to a lake with a cup and sitting by its side praying to it to fill the cup with water. You may sit there for a thousand years but it is certain that unless you lean forward and dip the cup into the water yourself nothing will happen. Even then you have to make certain that the cup is not already full of a lot of residue. Most cups are!

You say: "If there is nothing, why write?"

Yes, why? The whole thing can be summed up in four words: 'There is nothing, BE!' When one understands those four words one understands everything including Bhagavan himself.

Then there is no more to say!

൦൭ ൮൦

# Uniqueness of Bhagavan

## Dr. T.M.P. Mahadevan

BHAGAVAN WAS UNIQUE. He was unique in that he was not unique. What struck even a casual visitor to the Ashram was Bhagavan's naturalness. He did not impress any one as if he were non-natural, even supra-natural. There was no affectation at all in Sri Ramana. Let me illustrate what I mean. In South India sadhus refer to themselves, while speaking, in the third person. They would say 'this was walking' or 'this wants to go there' while referring to themselves. They would not use the first person singular 'I'. But Bhagavan quite naturally used to say 'I go', 'I walk', 'I sit' and so on. One who has the experience of the plenary illumination constantly, naturally, has no use for such affectations. And always he used to behave in the most natural manner. There was nothing which would make others think that there was some unnaturalness about Bhagavan.But yet once in his presence there was no need for prompting from outside. One would be convinced in one's own heart that one was in the presence of the non-dual Reality. Now, this was an experience that almost everyone had in the presence of Bhagavan.

He was an open book for all at all times. He did not make any distinction between what is private and what is public. So far as Bhagavan was concerned, there was no privacy. In those days, devotees used to be with him in the small meditation hall all day and night. We used to sleep in the same hall where we used to sit during daytime. And he was a silent witness to all that happened around him. Any one could walk in at any time. He was easily accessible not only to humans but also to animals. Squirrels used to play with him. The cow Lakshmi used to walk in at her own pleasure. The monkeys used to come into the Ashram without any let or hindrance. Bhagavan remarked about a trespassing cow, "Who is to be taken to task? If you had no fence and the cow walked in through your garden, who was responsible for this, you or the cow?"

Bhagavan's love and grace knew no limits. In his presence there was no high and no low. All were the same. There was no distinction between a Maharaja of old days who visited him and the rustics who wanted to have his *darshan.* He could understand the language of the mute creation. In earlier days when he was on the Hill Arunachala, the monkeys used to go to him for arbitration. This shows how Bhagavan taught the plenary experience to others — the experience which makes no distinction between one level of creation and another.

Others might think that Bhagavan practised austerities during the early years of his stay in Arunachala, that his *Mauna,* silence, was deliberate, that his sitting posture for days and weeks in the sub-terranean temple was *sadhana,* but some of us have heard him say that all this was not *tapasya,* although it seemed to be so. The time factor did not enter into the realisation of Bhagavan. There was no earlier preparation; there was no evolution thereafter. Of what is referred to in Advaita as *sadyomukti,* instantaneous release, we had a glowing example in Bhagavan Sri Ramana. One does not know what led to this instantaneous illumination. There was no growth, no procedural technique, no yogic meditation, no other *sadhana*. All of a sudden, the experience came without his inviting it. Now, this is unique; the entire history of sagehood holds no parallel. A boy at school who had no particular interest in spirituality, who was not even a brilliant boy in studies, that such a lad should, all of a sudden, become transformed into a sage, I think, is unique.And what was the nature of the realisation? It admitted no stages, required no effort. It was all complete. Completeness, fulness was there when Sri Ramana had in a trice solved the mystery of death. Nachiketas had to go to Yama, wait at his house for three days and nights, and put to him questions. The fear of death was only an occasion for solving the mystery. The non-dual Self which knows no death and no birth came to Sri Ramana in a flash; but that did not vanish like a flash, it remained as His *sahajasthiti*.

I am not saying that the process of meditation has no place in *sadhana,* but that what one gains through the method of thought-control, emptying of mind, is not the plenary experience of the non-dual *Atman*. In the case of Bhagavan this pinnacle was gained without the least conscious effort. That is his uniqueness. Ordinarily, a study of scripture comes first and then experience. But in the case of Bhagavan, experience came first and only later an acquaintance with what scriptures teach. It was when scholarly devotees came to him and wanted some doubt or other to be cleared that he listened to the readings from scriptures and then told them that His own experience confirmed what the texts taught.

The great scholars, both traditional and modern, were astounded at the simple words that fell from the lips of Bhagavan. Ganapati Sastri was one instance. He was a master of Sanskrit.

He was a great teacher. He practised *mantra-sadhana* all through his life. He was accepted as a *Guru* by a large number of disciples. But he was tormented and went to Sri Ramana. It was Ganapati Muni that announced to the world the greatness of Sri Ramana, finding the culmination of his earlier *sadhana* in Bhagavan.

Elsewhere, I have tried to compare these three great teachers of *Advaita:* Dakshinamurti, Sankara and Ramana. Dakshinamurti is the *Adi Guru,* the first preceptor. He sat beneath the banyan tree, a youthful figure surrounded by elderly disciples, and instructed them in the language of silence. Most of us cannot understand the language of silence. So, Dakshinamurti rose from His seat beneath the banyan tree and broke His silence. He appeared in the form of Sankaracarya. He is constantly going around this world, rousing it from its slumber.

All the great ones who came after him, whether they would acknowledge it openly or not, are but reflections of this form of Sankara. In the form of various masters it is Sankara that is moving in this world. It is the same Sankara that appeared to us as Sri Ramana.

The times have changed. The present world can be saved neither by the *Guru* who is seated in a particular place nor by the one who is perpetually moving about. The *Guru* who is required for our times is neither the one who keeps absolute silence, nor the one who, speaks profusely. We had this need satisfied in the *avatara* of Sri Ramana. He did not move out of the limits of Arunachala. He did not talk profusely or read extensively. Day in and day out, most of the time, he was in silence. People used to come with long lists of perplexing questions formulated in their minds; some of them, lest they might forget, used to write out those questions. But what happened? When they came and sat before Bhagavan they forgot all about those questions. I happened to be present when Paul Brunton came. P. B. had seen other saints in India. He had written out the questions which he wanted to ask. He sat there for a long time without opening his mouth. The friend who had come with him had to prompt him. It was only then that he read out his questions. This was not an isolated instance. This was the daily experience. The questioning mind was silenced in his presence.

And what is the quantum of his "writings"? But they are so potent that even a single line could transform the lives of people. Here, we have a middle course between silence and speech. Silently but surely the influence of Bhagavan is felt. No one could have thought some years ago that the influence would be felt so strongly in the capital of our country. But this is what is now happening all over the world. In Europe and America there are seekers, who when they get even a glimpse of Bhagavan's teachings feel that they have turned a new leaf in their lives.

What is, again, significant in Bhagavan's teaching is that it involves no mystification. There is nothing by way of creed. It is an open book of wisdom from which one could draw according to one's capacity. There is no narrowness or parochialism of any sort in the Master's teachings.

All the teachings of all the sages are put in a capsule form in this single sloka, *Hridayakuhara-madhye* which says that in the cave of the heart *Brahman* shines. He made known to *sadhakas* the *bardavidya*. He was the one who discovered that the spiritual heart is the Self itself. The *hridaya* is the non-dual spiritual Self. The 'I' is manifest in the region of the heart. When a person refers to himself he points to the right side of the chest. The 'I' shines in the heart; the Self is manifest in the cave of the heart. This manifestation of the Self in the form of 'I' is direct, immediate to every one. It does not require any belief, or faith or creed. One need not read *Sastra* to realise it, one realises it every moment: And the *Upanishads* tell us that in deep sleep one goes into it. Thus, one cannot deny oneself however much one might try. In a famous verse Sankara says "It is this 'I' which is immediately, directly experienced in the region of the heart by every one;" but this Self is not realised to be the non-dual *Brahman* on account of ignorance. There is no realising the Self. Because the Self is real, you cannot realise or make it real. What is to be done is to unrealise the unreal. We imagine that this world is real, while in fact it is not. Today the scientists are approaching Vedanta through science. Nuclear physics tells us that even in the hardest piece of matter there is no hardness. If you can accept the evidence of the physicist that what you regard as a concrete piece of matter is not concrete after all, then from a higher level is there anything which is unintelligible or impossible in the proclamation of the Sage that the entire world is Maya? Maya does not mean that there is no reality. In fact, the Self is the real and the world is only an appearance. And so, Bhagavan tells us that this *Aham-sphurana*, the 'I'-manifestation, is a pointer that, if we are judicious enough to discern the truth, we shall realise the identity of the Self with *Brahman*. This is what we have to experience. Self-realisation is no more than this. It is losing the individuality in the non-dual Reality. How is one to gain this? What is the way? *Hrdi visa*. Enter into the heart. Use the mind, but there is a stage where you have to transcend the mind and be what you are always. You can throw off your body; it is difficult to throw off your mind. It is with you all the time you are empirically conscious. You have to make use of it. It is in *jagrat* that you have to perform the *sadhana* not in deep sleep. We have to work this out during our conscious moments, moments of wakefulness. And what functions in wakefulness is the mind, which is to be made use of. Enter into the heart with your mind. The direct road is Self-enquiry. It is by Self-enquiry that you have to reach the heart. But if that becomes impossible for the moment, then adopt the technique of surrender. If even for this your mind is not ready, practise *pranayama*. You begin at the physical, vital level. Bhagavan says in the *Upadesa Saram* that the source of both the vital principle and the mind is the same. By controlling the vital principle you can control the mind. Begin then with the practice of regulating the breath.

You will find the mind settling down through the practice of *pranayama*, and then you will be ready for the right royal road. Very often people consider *jnana-yoga* to consist in intellectual analysis. This is not so. It is not intellectual speculation. Up to a point the mind can go; but there it stops. Bhagavan has taught a simple mode by which one goes beyond mind. What is that mode? The 'I'-thought is the first of all thoughts. All other thoughts arise after the I-thought. Only later on 'this', 'that' and 'the other' arise in your mind. Trace the source of the 'I'-thought and the practice will reveal to you that the 'I'-thought arises from the Self. Because we may not have either the competence or the time to go through the Sastras and discover the path ourselves, this technique is taught to us as it can be pursued by one and all at any time. This certainly is not an easy path. We must not delude ourselves by imagining that it is easy. It requires preparation, constant practice; it requires all the other *sadhanas*. But along with those *sadhanas* the enquiry can be practised. And if the Grace of the Guru is there, we will be helped on this road faster than we may imagine.

# THE MIRACULOUS AND SUPERNATURAL

## Marie B. Byles

TELEVISION ONCE SHOWED a picture of a man lying on his back on a bed of nails with two planks across him and a tractor or some-such thing being driven over him on the two planks; at one time a wheel slipped off the plank and went over his body. As he stood up the interviewer asked him how he did it and how he felt. He said that he put his faith in Almighty God and that he felt okay. Another film showed a man chewing up wine-glasses and saying he enjoyed eating them.

I cannot vouch personally for these two happenings. But it does seem that such strange and seemingly impossible things do occur with certain unusually gifted people, and that science is beginning to take notice of them and sometimes gives scientific explanations.

There are also the strange workings of astrology and psycho-kinesis — as when a tensed hand is held over a compass and swings the needle in the opposite direction, and extra-sensory perceptions — as when the details of the sinking of S.S. *Titanic* were perceived thousands of miles away at the same time that it happened. And most envied of all are the miracles of healing both physical and mental. There have always been many such healers, One of the best known is Agnes Sanford who wrote the well known *Healing Light*. And a less known mental healer was the American Buddhist monk, Sumangalo, who unexpectedly found he had suddenly acquired the ability to cure mental disorders. Among these apparent miracle-workers we must place those gifted preachers who have the power to convert people from delinquency and drug addiction.

Let us then admit that these supernormal happenings are factual, and also that science is becoming increasingly interested, so that we may well expect a widening of our knowledge.

The question we need to consider is whether it will make any difference to our social well-being if there are people trained to eat glass or even to cure people of drug addiction and delinquency. No supernormal talent in itself implies simple goodness and compassion which alone can bring about more harmonious relations between man and nature. True, some religious books assume the goodness of the healer and other miracle-workers, and assume that no one can be a saint unless he performs miracles. But are miracles any different from other supernormal happenings? Does what you call it make any difference? Those who now walk on fire for the edification of tourists, admit that it does not mean the same for them as it did when they performed the same act for the glory of God. But the fact remains that they outwardly achieve the same result as when they did do it for the glory of God. Those who examine these supernormal happenings from the scientific angle assume that the moral goodness of the doer has nothing to do with the matter.

And indeed — why should we think that goodness or badness in the doer is important? After all the world is composed of and founded upon pairs of opposites. Therefore we cannot have white magic without black magic too, any more than we can have a positive without a negative. It is therefore obvious that a person who performs, say, a miracle of healing is not necessarily a good man or woman. For this reason it may or may not be inspiring to read about miracles or other abnormal happenings, which appear to be supernatural.

The supernormal happening depends upon the natural talent of the individual who performs it. It is not of any importance. The only thing that matters is whether it springs from love and compassion which alone can draw us above the pairs of opposites. To read of those who performed no miracles, but who did achieve this love and compassion is far more likely to be helpful and inspiring to ordinary people like ourselves.

Foremost among such ordinary people of whose thoughts we have a written record is the saintly Stoic emperor of Rome in the second century, Marcus Aurelius, who kept a record of his meditations. And that simple record has been the inspiration of millions all over the world. And yet he had no outstanding talents. He had only simple goodness and kindness, springing from compassionate love and understanding of the oneness of all creation.

And another such was the simple Carmelite monk, Brother Lawrence of the 17th century, who performed no miracles except what the Buddha would call the only real miracle, that of a transformed life. He accomplished this merely by turning his mind to God and doing nothing but for the love of God. His whole being radiated serenity and love, and without any intellectual explanations his example transformed the lives of many.

Of course we must all use the talents we have been given and do the work that falls to our lot — being the emperor of a mighty empire, a cook in a monastery-kitchen, performer of miracles or healer of the sick. None is superior or inferior, and talents do not count The way to compassion and enlightenment is the same for all. We cannot and should not want to acquire supernatural talents we do not already possess, nor scientific knowledge beyond our normal capacity, nor even an inclination to harness these supernatural happenings or miracles. There are always specialists dealing with their particular fields. But we each have a built-in computer, as it were, which collects what is necessary for each of us according to our talents, if only we will let it work freely unimpeded by our predilections. One of the best ways of letting it work freely is to repeat in thought, or if possible in a whisper, what the Hindus would call a *mantra*, suited to one's individuality. Brother Lawrence's practice of the presence of God is a perfect example, for he would do nothing except for the love of God. By this means our whole being tends to get tuned-in with Cosmic laws and the harmony of the universe, whether we know them clearly or not.

Thus our individual talents get utilized by the internal computer and get directed as migratory birds and fishes are. Then whatever our talent, whether to perform operations without anaesthetics like the Philippine healers, or merely to wash dishes, our work will be well done.

Therefore let us read and learn whatever is helpful, but let us not be bewildered by or crave for supernormal powers. Let us be content with the Inner Light that has been given to us, remembering that the greatest of Masters like Buddha, Ramakrishna Paramahamsa and Ramana have decried the craving for and display of supernormal powers as utterly detrimental to one's spiritual enlightenment.

ଓ ๒

# AN ANGRY PRAYER

## Jean Butler

*In this moving narrative we see the efficacy of an intense prayer.*

SOME YEARS AGO my daughter Martha and I were living on the island of St. Croix in the Caribbean. At that time the Virgin Islands (in which group this falls) were so poverty-stricken that they were spoken of as the world's poorhouse.

One evening I went into the local drug store and found the chemist, Mr. Edwards, arguing in English with a little Puerto Rican peasant who was pleading volubly with him in Spanish.

Mr. Edwards was saying, "I'm sorry I can't give you any credit. I don't own the drug store. I am only an employee and have to obey orders."

The peasant answered, "It is only until my tomatoes are harvested. Then I can pay you."

Mr. Edwards was unmoved.

"But," cried the peasant in despair, "what will my son do without the medicine?" At that point I said rather angrily, "Give him the medicine, Mr. Edwards, and put it on my bill."

I turned to the peasant and asked what was the matter with his son. A torrent of Spanish poured forth as he explained. He had five children ranging from fourteen years to three months. His wife had died giving birth to the baby. The oldest boy had epileptic fits, as many as five a day. By law the children had to go to school, but when the eldest boy had his medicine he could stay at home in the mornings and take care of the baby while the father worked his land. If the boy did not have his medicine he could not be left with the baby. Nor could he go to school. The only thing the father could do was to tie the baby on to his back when he went to work on his land and leave the boy unattended in the house; and on one such occasion the boy had a fit during which he broke his leg.

A wave of such intense fury, pity and sheer horror came over me that for a moment I turned dizzy — not only on account of the little peasant but also of all the others in the world who were equally suffering and equally hopeless and helpless.

I told the peasant that I knew a great specialist in New York to whom I would write for a new medicine I had been reading about. I wrote down the peasant's name and the age and weight of his son. "The medicine should come in about ten days," I said, "and I will have it sent care of Edwards for you."

I rushed out into the night blind and sick with rage against God. "D—n you!"

I cried, "What are you doing? Why don't you at least help the poor and sick who can do nothing to help themselves and who have nothing?" I cried and cursed all the way up the long hill to my house, hating the world, hating God, hating the unspeakable injustice of life. All night, even in my sleep I alternated prayers with curses and invectives and blind anger. Day and night for a week I had no peace. I directed my thoughts repeatedly to the sick boy, saying to him, "God made you in His image and likeness. God is perfect, without flaw or sickness. Be you therefore perfect, as your Father in heaven is perfect.

That is what Christ said to you." This alternated with my repeating that, "not even a sparrow falls to the ground without His knowing it." And I pointed out somewhat bitterly that the Son of God had said, "Inasmuch as you do it to one of the least of these you do it also to me."

Gradually the anger and frenzy died down, but remembrance of the peasant and his epileptic son continued day and night. One evening, about ten days after my first meeting with the peasant, I was just going into the drug-store when a bare-footed man in worn overalls and a big straw hat came out, holding a package in one hand. On seeing me he swept off his hat, waved the package in the air and exclaimed excitedly, "This has just come, the medicine for my son. But I no longer need it. Something has happened."

It was the same peasant. I had not recognized him with his hat on. I knew what was coming and felt faint because of it. I said, "Remember, Senor, the Bible says that the Lord giveth and the Lord taketh away. What He does is a mystery to us. Don't ask any questions. Just go to the church and give thanks to God."

"But Senora," he said, "I must tell you what has happened. Since we talked the other night my son has had no more fits. What shall I do with this?" And he held out the box of medicine.

I had known what was coming. "Don't open it, Senor," I said, "You won't need it. Just go to the church and give thanks to God." And I turned and rushed up the hill to my house, thinking, "Excuse me, God! Forgive me!", consumed with humility and shame at my former rage, overflowing with love of God.

On a Sunday morning some months later, when I had completely forgotten the peasant and his son, I was leaving my house with Martha to go to the beach when an ancient truck full of people dressed in their Sunday best came roaring up the hill and stopped outside my door. One by one they scrambled out and came on to the terrace, each one carrying something in his hand. They made quite a pile there — fruit, eggs, chickens, fish, freshly baked bread, a bottle of wine, lobsters — and then they returned to the truck, while I kept on remonstrating, "You have made a mistake! You have come to the wrong house! I didn't order anything!"

Just then my little Puerto Rican friend, scarcely recognizable in his Sunday clothes, came up to me shyly and said, "Senora, these are my relatives. We have brought you these gifts to show our appreciation for what you did for my son."

"But Senor", I protested, "I did nothing, nothing! Please try to understand me. It was not I who did it!"

Then I asked him about his son, how he was now. He glowed with quiet pride. "He has gained fifteen pounds," he said, "he is quite well now. I sent him to the island of St. Thomas to work on his uncle's farm for a few weeks and now he is back here with me. He works on the land with me in the morning and we earn enough to pay a girl to look after the baby, and in the afternoons he goes to school. He has never had another fit."

CB EO

# AN INCARNATE ABBOT EXPLAINS

*Asked about reincarnation, Sri Bhagavan remarked, "See how a tree grows again when its branches are cut off. So long as the life source is not destroyed it will grow. Similarly, latent potentialities withdraw into the heart at death but do not perish. That is how beings are reborn." Here is an instance taken from a speech by Trungpa Trulku Rinpoche given at Roselaleham.*

AFTER THE DEATH of the previous Abbot of Surmang, my monastery, the monks sent a deputation to His Holiness Gyalwa Karmapa, the head of our particular school of Tibetan Buddhism. They asked him whether he could tell them where their Abbot had taken birth again, so that they could bring him back among them. Gyalwa Karmapa spent several days in meditation, and finally gave them the answer that their Abbot was born as a young child living in the village of Geje, in a house facing south and that the family had two children and a brown dog. After some difficulty the monks found the house and the young child, who was myself.

I am told that as the monks came in and presented me with the traditional white scarf, I behaved in exactly the right manner, although I had never been taught how. Also that I recognised various objects that had been the possessions of my predecessor, shown to me among others of the same kind. Eventually they were convinced that I was the eleventh Abbot Trungpa and they brought me back to Surmang.

Shortly after that I was formally enthroned as Abbot, although of course, all my duties were performed by an elder monk acting as regent. I was put into the charge of a tutor, and continued to see my parents from time to time. I began learning about religion from my tutor, who told me about the life of Gautama the Buddha and about his teachings. At the age of eight I began my first simple meditation.

From then on I learned more and more about the various meditations of our school. I received instruction from two of the great Gurus or Teachers of Eastern Tibet. One of them, Chentse Rinpoche, is now in India and is still my Guru. Sometimes I lived in the monastery and sometimes away from it, in retreat. Every monk of our school spends several years in solitary meditation during that time, living, sleeping and eating in one small room. Meditation is really the heart of a monk's life, for in it he discovers and experiences the actual truth of the teachings he has before known only intellectually. I do not want to speak about the particular techniques of meditation. There are many and they are adapted to suit the needs of all kinds of individuals. I want rather to speak about the reasons for meditation and its essence, for meditation is not necessarily a matter of sitting cross-legged and motionless for long periods of time, it is something that may be practised, consciously or unconsciously by anyone at any time.

You will be able to draw parallels to what I shall say both from the beliefs and practices of other religions and from your own experiences. We are all human beings and our existence presents similar problems and similar possibilities. As Milarepa, the great sage and poet of Tibet, sang from the top of mountains, 'I am the goal of every great meditator, I am the meeting place of the faithful, I am the coil of birth, death and decay.'

To start at the beginning — each one of us may be struck at one time or another by the inadequacy of our way of experiencing the world. We feel that something is missing, that our attempts to explain and to organise our lives and to provide ourselves with an emotional security are doomed to failure and are indeed in themselves contradictory to the nature of things. Also that in our simply fulfilling our own desires we are cheating the Universe.

Meditation is the attempt to remove those aspects of our natures in which our awareness of life is limited and confined, and experience a new depth. Upon what does our everyday picture of the world depend? It depends not upon things themselves but on our reactions to them. We project outwards on things our own hopes and prejudices, and order our separate world accordingly. Meditation is a gradual loss of these private worlds, and realisation that our true natures lie hidden in the heart of the Universe.

It is one of the fundamental teachings of Buddhism that things in themselves are without substance. They are all, like flowers, springing up suddenly out of nothingness and again withering. The world of things, or the appearance of things, is a kind of puppet show, a masquerade. In itself it possesses a kind of demonic energy, but it can give no lasting satisfaction to the heart. In meditation we begin to cross the threshold between appearance and reality.

Many of us will have thought like this, but will also have experienced how difficult this threshold is to cross. All unconsciously, the world of appearances exercises a certain fascination. Everything in its appearances releases a small charge of energy, and our ignorant minds, feeling dissatisfaction with their existing states, leap to swallow this charge. Thereafter, the imprint of the object remains fixed in the memory. If the experience is in some way pleasurable, the mind desires a repetition of it. If it is unpleasant, the mind will reject any repetition of it, and a negative force is set up.

Meditation consists of seeing the world for precisely what it is. This can be done only when one remains quite unaffected by hatred or desire. One observes dispassionately one's reactions to things, and gradually the passions of greed and hatred are driven out of one's system. Instead of reaching out for one thing after another, one becomes calmer and more self-possessed. One uses the strength thus released to gradually eliminate distracted and discursive thoughts as they arise, and brings oneself into a state of clear, one-pointed awareness. One begins to experience greater freedom and room to move about. One no longer heeds one's hopes and fears, and lets go the burden of them. Becoming nothing, one becomes everything and suddenly it may happen that one is left for a moment still. There is before one, through one and around one infinite space — the reality flowing unobstructed. As Milarepa says:

'As happy as the current of a great river,
So is the sage who enjoys the stream of thought.'

This is possible for everyone, but clearly it requires certain qualities in us, and it requires time to come to fruition.

We need first of all to have clearly in our minds what we are trying to do. Our basic assumptions influence us far more than we realise and we must become thoroughly steeped in the ideas and the attitudes of the spiritual life before we can begin. I had to memorise a large portion of our scriptures and repeat them by heart to my tutor.

As well as study, we need determination and integrity. Each one stands before the threshold of eternity, alone with himself. He cannot rely on any created thing. Each one of us can forge a true vessel only out of himself; others may help us but in the end it is we alone who are responsible. Gradually we have to realise the agony of our mistakes, our failure to understand and we have to have the courage to come out of prison.

Beyond this solitude, one thing else is needed. Just as everything in the world of appearance releases a charge of energy, so also does everything in eternity. That energy, indeed, is far stronger because it has been purified of the stain of greed, hatred and material illusion. The thought is not a thought of anything, it is a thought which in itself is pure energy, passing into and through everything unobstructed. So when we purify our minds, a force is built up from which each one of us can draw and in the light of which, each one can examine himself. In the monasteries and hermitages of Tibet I could feel this strength in operation. It was something of which we were all part. If I may be allowed to say so, I feel this atmosphere lacking in the cities and even in many churches of this country. I hope very much that during our time here together, we may join in making a spirit that one may call new and some may call old but which in itself abides forever.

CB 80

# ZEN STORIES

*The following are well-known specimens of Zen stories, much condensed.*

TWO MONKS, one older, one young, came to a muddy ford where a pretty girl was waiting to cross. The elder picked her up and carried her over the water. As they went along, the younger, horrified at the act of his brother monk in touching a woman, kept on commenting upon it, until at last the elder exclaimed: "What! Are you still carrying that girl? I put her down as soon as we crossed the water!"

\* \* \*

When a Master was troubled by a monk who persisted in saying that he could not understand, the Master said: "Come nearer." The monk came nearer. The Master again said: "Come nearer," and once more the monk did so. "How well you understand!" remarked the Master!

\* \* \*

A boastful monkey went to heaven and there met the Buddha. He said: "Buddha is a small thing, but I can jump many leagues." "If you are so clever," said the Buddha, "jump away from the palm of my hand." The monkey thought that would be easy since the palm seemed to him only inches wide. So he leaped far, far away. He found himself on a large plain bounded by five great pillars. To prove he had been there he made a mark at the base of one of these. After returning to Buddha he boasted of what he had done. "But look at my hand," said Buddha. There the monkey saw the mark which he had made. It was at the base of one of Buddha's fingers!

\* \* \*

A Master was once approached by a boy requesting instruction, so the Master gave him the *koan*: "What is the sound of the clapping of one hand?" The boy went away and happened to hear some Geishas playing, so he went to the Master and imitated that. On being told that was not it, he went away and heard water dripping, again the water flowing, again the locust — altogether ten times. All were wrong. Then the boy could find or think of no more, and lo! he discovered the soundlessness of one hand, the sound of sound!

\* \* \*

A man chased by a tiger jumped over a cliff and clung to a tree growing on the side. Looking down he saw another tiger waiting for him to fall. Worse and worse, he saw two mice, one white and one black, gnawing at the branch to which he was clinging. It chanced that he just then caught sight of some strawberries growing within reach. With one hand he plucked a strawberry and put it in his mouth. "How good it tastes!" he thought.

\* \* \*

A Zen monk named Ryoken lived in a hut alone and without any possessions. One day when he was out, a thief entered to steal. He was about to depart when the monk returned. The monk said: "I am sorry you have found nothing; please take my clothes." After the thief had gone, the monk sat naked looking at the moon. "Alas!", he mused, "What a pity that I could not give him that beautiful moon!"

# THE STORY OF LILA

*An elderly gentleman, formerly a co-worker with B. V. Narasimhaswami and author of some Visishtadvaita work, visited the place for the first time. He asked about rebirths, if it is possible for the linga sarira (subtle body) to get dissolved and be reborn two years after death.*

*M.: Yes. Surely. Not only can one be reborn, one may be twenty or forty or even seventy years old in the new body though only two years after death.*

*Sri Bhagavan cited Lila's story from Yoga Vasishta.*

*(Talk No.129)*

There was a reference to reincarnation. Reincarnation of Shanti Devi tallies with the human standards of time whereas the latest case reported of a boy of seven is different. The boy is seven years now. He recalls his past births. Enquiries go to show that the previous body was given up 10 months ago.

The question arises how the matter stood for six years and two months previous to the death of the former body. Did the soul occupy two bodies at the same time?

Sri Bhagavan pointed out that the seven years is according to the boy and the ten months is according to the observer. The difference is due to these two different *upadhis* (mental states). The boy's experience extending to seven years has been calculated by the observer to cover only 10 months of his own time.

Sri Bhagavan again referred to Lila's story in *Yoga Vasishta*. (Talk No.261)

Once there was a king by the name of Padma, who was wealthy and wise. He had a beautiful wife called Lila who was devoted to her husband. Once she thought, "My Husband is dearer to me than my life. He is young and prosperous. How to make him remain forever young and deathless?"

She consulted learned pandits of the court. They advised her, "All successful accomplishments are attained by religious austerity, repetition of *mantras* and self-control, but immortality can not be obtained on any account."

Having heard thus from the learned Brahmins, she reflected, "In case I have to die before my husband, freed from all agony, I shall happily rest in the Self and in case he precedes me then his soul should not go out of this room. I shall worship the Goddess Sarasvati and ask for boons."

Having resolved thus the queen, without telling her husband, performed severe austerities as laid down in the scriptures.

Goddess Sarasvati was pleased by the queen's austerities. She appeared and said, "Ask for any boon and it shall be granted." Overjoyed Lila sang hymns of praise to the Goddess, and asked for two boons: "When my husband dies, the soul of my husband, should remain here. Whenever I pray to you, give me your vision." Accordingly, the Goddess granted both the boons.

After several years Lila's husband passed away. The bereaved queen placed her husband's corpse in a bed of flowers as instructed by the Goddess. In great distress she asked the Goddess, "Where does my husband reside? What does he do? What is his state at present? Lead me to him. I cannot live without him."

The Goddess taught Lila about Brahman (the Supreme Spirit or Ultimate Reality) and narrated the existence of various planes penetrating one another and existing quite unperceived by the inhabitants of other planes. She also taught her the method of seeing and visiting the various worlds interpenetrating one's own. Lila abandoned her own body, and the Goddess took her to the world of her husband's in which she saw him in an assembly of kings. She was surprised to see him sitting on a throne, now looking very young. Lila asked the Goddess for an explanation. She was told about the delusion of creation. The Goddess spoke as follows:

"Once there lived a virtuous Brahmin named Vasishta. His wife was Arundhati who equalled him in all respects. Once he saw the king passing by with his retinue and thought, 'Kingship is indeed delightful, blessed with all good fortune. I wish that I were a king.'

"Vasishta's death was impending and knowing this, his wife took refuge in me. Like you, she prayed to me, 'May the soul of my dead husband not depart from this place.' I granted her prayer. The poor Brahmin died, his wife, Arundhati, being unable to bear the pangs of separation from her husband, burnt herself along with the body of her husband." Sarasvati told Lila that all that had happened only a week ago, and that the Brahmin pair had been born as herself (Lila) and her husband, King Padma, in the world where he had just died after having lived a long life, leaving Lila alone. Lila did not believe this story, because the couple had died recently, whereas Lila and Padma were born years before. Lila asked the Goddess whether one soul can occupy two bodies simultaneously. Saraswati explained that the two frames of reference were different and that a person's strong *sankalpa* (determination or aspiration) can manifest as humans.

The Goddess then took Lila to that world, and made her verify the story from a son of the deceased pair. Through meditation, she remembered all her previous births since her origin from the Creator. Lila lamented, "Alas! Today I have remembered hundreds of my previous births. Indeed, I have wandered much in various kinds of wombs."

Both Lila and Sarasvati returned to the present world of the king, who was called Viduratha, and found him in his 70th year. His wife was also named Lila (let us call her Lila II). Lila and Saraswati manifested themselves before the king in his private apartment and mysteriously reminded him of his previous existence as Padma. He entertained a desire to be Padma again. His present wife, Lila II, propitiated Sarasvati to confer a boon upon her to be the wife of Viduratha even in his next life.

After a short time, there was a war in which King Viduratha was killed. His soul, which was present, throughout, in the room where the corpse of Padma was lying, reentered the dead body. And lo! The soul rose again as King Padma, who found standing before him his two wives, namely, Lila I and Lila II. "Let all sorrows end and let there be endless happiness." So saying the Goddess blessed them and disappeared.

Finally, all three of them — Lila, the second Lila and the King — were liberated while still alive, and in due course, became one with the Absolute by the grace of the Goddess.

 C3 80

# APPENDIX

## Important Events in Sri Bhagavan's Life

**1879** December 30, Monday – corresponding to 16, *Margali* of Tamil Year *Pramadi* – Star *Punarvasu* – *Ardra Darshan* Day – Born at 1 a.m. at Tiruchuli ('Sri Sundara Mandiram').

**1891** Moves to Dindigul, after completing elementary education at Tiruchuli.

**1892** February 18: Death of father, Sundaram Iyer. Moves to Madurai. Studies at Scott's Middle School and American Mission High School.

**1895** November: Hears of 'Arunachala' mentioned to him by an elderly relative.

**1896** (about middle of July): 'Death Experience' at Madurai ending in complete and permanent Realisation of the Self ('*Sri Ramana Mandiram*').
August 29, Saturday: Leaves Madurai for Arunachala.
September 1 – Tuesday: Arrives in Arunachala – Stays in the Temple premises within the Thousand-pillared Hall, beneath the *Illupai* Tree, in *Pathala Linga* (underground cellar), sometimes in the *Gopuram*.

**1897** Moves to Gurumurtam in the outskirts of the town (early in the year).
Stays in the shrine and the adjoining Mango grove.

**1898** May: Uncle Nelliappa Iyer visits Bhagavan at Mango grove.
September: Moves to Pavalakkunru.
December: Mother Alagammal visits Bhagavan at Pavalakkunru.

**1899** February: Moves to the Hill, Arunachala. Stays in various caves up the Hill, but mostly in Virupaksha Cave, using Mango Tree Cave as summer residence.

1900 Replies to questions put by Gambiram Seshayya, at Virupaksha Cave.

1902 *(*The above published as *Self-enquiry)*

1902 Answers to questions asked by Sivaprakasam Pillai *(Who am I?).*

1905 Moves to Pachaiamman Koil for six months during the plague epidemic — returns to the Hill.

1907 November 18: Momentous meeting between Bhagavan and Kavyakanta Ganapati Muni. Bhagavan imparts *upadesa* to Muni.

1908 (January to March): Stays at Pachaiamman Koil (with Ganapati Muni and others) and again goes back to Virupaksha Cave.
Translates into Tamil prose Adi Sankara's *Viveka Chudamanai* and *Drik Drisya Viveka.*

1911 November: F.H. Humphreys, the first Westerner, meets Bhagavan.

1912 Second death experience at Tortoise Rock in the presence of Vasudeva Sastry and others.

1914 Offers prayers (songs) to Arunachala for Mother's recovery from illness.

1915 The *Song of the Pappadum* written for the sake of mother. The following were also written during Virupaksha days: *Arunachala Aksharamanamalai, Arunachala Padikam, Arunachala Ashtakam,* Translation of *Devi Kalottara,* Translation of Adi Sankara's *Hymn to Dakshinamurti, Guru Stuti* and *Hastamalaka Stotra.*

1916 Moves to Skandashram.

1917 Composes *Arunachala Pancharatnam* in Sanskrit. Mother settles at Skandashram. *Sri Ramana Gita* in Sanskrit written by Ganapati Muni.

1922 May 19, Friday: Mother's *Maha Samadhi.*

Middle of December: Moves to the present site of *Sri Ramanasramam.*

**1927** Composes *Upadesa Sara* in Tamil, Telugu, Sanskrit and Malayalam.

April 24: Composes *Atma Vidya* (Self Knowledge).

**1928** Composes *Ulladu Narpadu* (Forty Verses on Reality) in Tamil and Malayalam (*Sat Darshanam*).

**1930** *Sat Darshanam* in Sanskrit (translated from Tamil by Ganapati Muni).

**1933** Translated into Tamil the *Agama: Sarvajnanotharam – Atma Sakshatkara.*

**1939** September 1, Thursday: Foundation laid by Bhagavan for the Matrubhuteswara Temple.

**1940** Selects 42 verses from *The Bhagavad Gita* (now entitled The Song Celestial) and translates them into Tamil and Malayalam.

**1947** February: Composes *Ekatma Panchakam* (Five Verses on the Self) in Telugu and Tamil.

**1948** June 18: Cow Lakhsmi attains *Nirvana.*

Translates into Tamil *Atma Bodha* of Adi Sankara.

**1949** March 17, Thursday – *Kumbabhishekam* of Matrubhuteswara Temple in the presence of Bhagavan.

**1950** April 14, Friday: *Brahma Nirvana* of Bhagavan at 8-47 p.m. At that moment a shooting star, vividly luminous, coming from the South (the present *Nirvana* Room) and moving slowly northward across the sky and disappearing behind the peak of Arunachala was observed by many in various parts of India.

৩ ৪০